FREEDOM
FROM FEAR

FREEDOM

FROM FEAR

TRAVIS BURKE

**Foreword by
Dr. Bill Basansky**

Freedom From Fear
Copyright © 2004 by Travis Burke

ISBN 0-9760738-0-3

Library of Congress Control Number: 2004112020

Published by:
Seed Word Communications
P.O. Box 16615
Tallahassee, FL 32317
Toll-Free: (866) 517-3872
Local: (850) 893-9781
www.SeedWord.com

Cover Design:
Gifted-Hands LifeStyle Center, Inc.
577 Hillandale Park Drive
Lithonia, GA 30058
Phone: (678) 418-6422

You may inquire about the audiobook version as well as the Spanish translation of this book.

Contents

Contents

Foreword

I am a firm believer that ANY person, Christian or non-Christian, who is constantly tormented in his mind and body must have hope and must know there are answers awaiting him somewhere. As you read this book, <u>Freedom From Fear</u>, written by Travis Burke, you will find your freedom from fear.

Especially valuable are two facets of this book: It is practical, covering true-to-life issues such as the nature of fear and the torment and destruction fear brings; and it has a strong biblical foundation. <u>Freedom From Fear</u> will teach you how you can live a good life *without* fear.

The bottom line is that this book will help you change the way you think, so you can change the way you live. <u>Freedom From Fear</u> is a book needed in the world in which we live today, and I highly recommend it to you.

Dr. Bill Basansky

Life International Church
PO Box 07459
Fort Myers, FL   33919

www.DrBillOnline.com

Recommendation

In times like these, with so much terrorism in the world, this book is a must for every library. Everyone should read it through more than once and should refer to it often. People operate either by the spirit of faith or they operate according to fear. This book will answer many questions you may have and will help you to get rid of some fears you have held on to for so many years.

I have known Pastors Travis and Caleta Burke for several years and am proud to recommend your purchase and reading of "Freedom From Fear." It will bless your life.

Rev. Clyde Oliver

Clyde Oliver Ministries Inc./ Maranatha Christian Center
Melbourne, Florida. USA

About the Author

Travis and Caleta Burke have an International Ministry based in Tallahassee, Florida, USA. They are the Senior Pastors of New Life International Outreach Center. At the heart of this ministry is a focus on faith in the Word of God and a desire to reach the world with the "Good News" of a victorious life in Christ.

In 1975, Travis and Caleta began their ministry as Associate Pastors and Pastors of various churches in Georgia and Florida. In 1982, God led Travis and Caleta to establish New Life International Outreach Center, a local ministry with a world vision. Their congregation is a beautiful combination of races and cultures that have come together to serve God as one body of believers.

New Life TV is a media outreach that Travis and Caleta established on a local TV station in 1995. It has since grown to a National TV Program seen in several million homes, twice weekly, on the Dish Network. The continuing outreach to the world includes the ministry's web-site: www.newlifetv.com

Travis and Caleta are featured conference speakers at National and International conventions. They have brought answers to many and continue to strive for excellence in ministry.

You may contact Pastors Travis and Caleta at:

New Life International Outreach Center
2633 Hartsfield Road
Tallahassee, Florida 32303
Phone: (850) 386-6129
E-Mail: newlifetv@cfaith.com

Foundational Scriptures

"For God has not given us the spirit of fear, but of power and of love and of a sound mind" (**2 Timothy 1:7**).

"There is no fear in love; but perfect love casts out fear, because fear involves torment. He who fears has not been made perfect in love" (**1 John 4:18**).

"Inasmuch then as the children have partaken of flesh and blood, He Himself likewise shared in the same, that through death He might destroy him who had the power of death, that is, the devil, and release those who through fear of death were all their lifetime subject to bondage" (**Hebrews 2: 14-15**).

"And in nothing be terrified by your adversaries: which is to them an evident token of perdition, but to you of salvation, and that of God" (**Philippians 1:28**).

"And do not for a moment be frightened or intimidated in anything by your opponents and adversary. For such consistency and fearlessness will be a clear sign and proof and seal to them of their impending destruction, but a sure token and evidence of your deliverance and salvation, and that from God" (**Philippians 1:28 AMP**).

Chapter 1

<u>Two Kinds Of Fear</u>

Two kinds of fear are mentioned in the Bible. One fear has torment but the other does not. The good kind of fear is the fear of the LORD. The bad kind of fear is the fear of Satan. Fear is reverence, high respect and honor.

> *"...the fear of the LORD is the beginning of knowledge: but fools despise wisdom and instruction, for that they hated knowledge, and did not choose the fear of the LORD. They would none of my counsel: they despised all my reproof. Therefore shall they eat of the fruit of their own way, and be filled with their own devices"* **(Proverbs 1: 7, 29-31).**

In the Book of Proverbs, God offered His children knowledge and wisdom, but they rejected it. They did not have the fear of the LORD. The absence of the fear of the LORD is the same as the presence of the fear of the devil. Evil is the opposite of good. There is no middle ground. You are either on the good side (the God side) or on the side of evil. If you do not have reverence, respect and honor for God, then it means you have reverence, respect and honor for the devil. In other words, if you do not have the fear of the LORD (the good fear), then you have the fear of the devil (the bad kind).

In Proverbs Chapter 1, instead of "reverence, respect and honor" for God, these people turned their reverence, respect and honor towards the devil. Instead of having "the fear of the LORD", they had "the fear of the devil." This is the bad kind of fear. The "fear of the devil" brings torment. When you have reverence, respect and honor toward your enemy, you will live a life of torment. The aim of this book is to expose the bad kind of fear – the fear of the devil. We will learn from scripture that God has delivered us from the bad kind of fear.

Unless otherwise qualified, when we use the word "fear" in this book, we are referring to the fear of the devil – the bad kind of fear. You may notice that some statements and Bible verses are repeated several times throughout the book. This is done on purpose to emphasize the importance of those statements and Bible references as they relate to our topic of fear.

This book is not designed to be a medical or psycho-analytical discussion on the topic of fear. The primary aim of the author is to expose the effects of the unhealthy fear of Satan in the lives of believers and non-believers alike.

Chapter 2

We Have Been Delivered From Fear

God has already delivered us from fear. The foundational verse in Hebrews 2 says that Jesus went through death, so that He might deliver them who were bound by the fear of death all through their lifetime.

Notice in **2 Timothy 1:7** that fear is a spirit. This verse does not simply refer to <u>a</u> spirit of fear but <u>the</u> spirit of fear. Fear is a personality. Fear doesn't just come by itself. There is a design behind fear. There is a source and master plan behind fear. Fear comes from only one source. The scripture says God is not the source of fear. God is a Spirit but not the spirit of fear. **2 Timothy 1:7** says God has given us the spirit of power, the spirit of love and the spirit of a sound mind. **Galatians 5:22** lists the fruit of the re-created spirit as love, joy, peace, patience, kindness, goodness, faithfulness, gentleness and self-control. Fear is not included in this list. Fear is not a part of the fruit of the spirit.

We know from scripture **(1 John 4:8)** that God is love. **1 John 4:18** says perfect love casts out fear. Light and darkness cannot co-exist in the same place at the same time. Perfect love and fear cannot dwell together in the same house. If God is love and love casts out fear, then fear must not be from God. Since the spirit of fear does not come from God, we must conclude that the personality and the source behind fear is the devil.

The good news in **Hebrews 2: 14-15** is that Jesus went through death so that He might destroy the devil and release us from bondage to fear. The devil <u>had</u> the power of death until Jesus took that power away from him. After we become born again, we need to realize that we are no longer in bondage to fear or to Satan. However, it is possible for us to remain in ignorance and not claim the freedom that has been provided for us through the death, burial and resurrection of our LORD Jesus Christ. The devil still <u>has</u> the power of death over those who are not born again.

Satan cannot get into our lives and overcome us unless we give him permission. The Bible says in **Ephesians 4:27** that we should not give any place to the devil. This means that the devil cannot have any place in us unless we give him that place. When the spirit of fear tries to attach itself to us and succeeds, then it means we have given him access or an open door in our lives. The devil cannot do anything in our lives unless we allow him to do it. The surprising truth is that even if someone is not born again, the devil still cannot do anything in that person's life unless he finds an open door.

Do you know that even God cannot do anything in our lives unless we give him permission? If it was all left to God, then all of us Christians will be prosperous and healthy because that is God's will for us. It is God's will for us to be healed *(3 John 2)*. The reason God sent His son to die on the cross was that we would be saved and healed. The Bible says, *"By His stripes, we are healed"* **(Isaish 53:5).** God wants to come into our lives and be a blessing to us but He chooses to wait until we give Him permission. See what God says in the Book of Revelation:

> *"Behold I stand at the door and knock. If anyone hears my voice and opens the door, I will come in to him and dine with him"* **(Revelation 3:20).**

So, neither God nor Satan can work in our lives without our permission. God is a good God. He only brings good things into your life. God wants to save you, deliver you, heal you and prosper you. But His hands are tied until you allow Him. The devil, on the other hand, wants to steal from you. He wants to kill you. He wants to destroy you. God tells us in **John 10:10** that *"the thief* (the devil) *does not come except to steal, and to kill, and to destroy. I* (God) *have come that they may have life and that they may have it more abundantly."*

Remember that neither God nor the devil can do anything in our lives unless we allow them. If it was all left to Satan, he would have destroyed all of us. Satan has absolutely no love for humanity. But he does not have free access into our lives unless we give it to him.

We learn from several scriptures that the way we allow God into our lives is through faith.

Faith comes to us by sowing the Word of God into our lives and watering that Word on a daily basis.

> *"Faith comes by hearing, and hearing by the Word of God"* **(Romans 10:17)**.

The more we develop our faith in God, the more we allow Him to show Himself strong in our lives. We let God into our lives through the door of faith.

The opposite of faith is fear. We let Satan into our lives through the door of fear. Faith comes by hearing the Word of God and fear comes by hearing the word of the devil. Fear is the door or path through which the devil enters into our lives and our affairs. We are going to see from the Bible that there is a way for us to shut the devil out. We will learn how to open the door for God to manifest Himself in our lives. We will also learn how to shut the door to fear and to Satan.

Everything doesn't just happen to us because we are in this world. We have more control than we realize over the things which happen in our lives. Our own choices determine how much good or bad things happen in our lives. We hold the keys that can open or lock the door to either God or Satan. A lot of Christians go through life asking "why?" Through our discussions in this book, we will get a better understanding and get the "whys" out of our lives.

Chapter 3

<u>The Nature of Fear</u>

I would like you to consider the following important facts about fear:

1. **Fear separates us from God.**

    We established earlier the fact that fear and perfect love cannot dwell together in the same house. Since God is love, fear and God cannot dwell together in our lives

2. **Fear causes disobedience.**

    As believers, we don't just disobey God. There is a reason for our disobedience. Fear is that reason.

3. **Fear is the path of Satan.**

    If you want to travel to a certain destination, you must have a path or road to get there. There is no way for the devil to get into your life unless he has a road. Fear is that road. Fear is the bridge that Satan travels on to get into your life. I will show you how to blow up that bridge and close that road. You will learn how to get rid of all the phobias in your life. You will not be afraid of heights. You can go up to any floor of any tall building without being afraid. You will be free from the fear of terrorism. You can fly on any airplane without the fear of being high-jacked or the plane crashing.

One old preacher was asked if he was going to fly to a certain destination. He said, "Oh, No, I'm going to obey the scripture." When they asked him what scripture, he said, God said, "<u>Low</u>, I will be with you always." Of course, we realize that this was meant to be a joke but it is misinterpreting the Bible and just an excuse for not dealing with this preacher's fear of flying. Some people are afraid of the dark, cats, dogs, snakes, rivers, the sea, rain, lightning, thunder and many different things. All these fears open the door and provide a path to Satan to enter our lives.

The devil will not come unless you invite him. After learning the facts from this book and discovering God's Word from the Bible, if you still invite the devil into your life, your business and your affairs, then you must blame yourself. There is a difference between ignorance and stupidity. If we do something wrong because we did not have the right information, then that is ignorance. But if we did that wrong thing after having the right information, then that is stupidity. I hope we will not be stupid after reading this book.

We need to realize also that the devil doesn't just wait patiently to be invited. He entices us in the areas he knows we are vulnerable in. He plays tricks on our minds to cause us to open the door. Sometimes, if we are not careful, we might not even remember when we opened that door. The devil is smart enough not to show up on the very same day that we allowed some fear into our lives.

We may be blaming God for allowing Satan into our lives when, in fact, it was our own fault.

If we discover that the devil has already entered into certain areas of our lives, we should admit that it is our fault and learn how to get rid of him. If you discover any such area in your life, please don't let pride prevent you from admitting it. All of us believers have failed at one time or another. The good news is that we do not have to just lie down and die in our failures. The Bible says in **Proverbs 24:16** that *"A righteous man may fall seven times, but he will rise again."* We are the righteousness of God in Christ. So we may fall seven times, but we will rise again.

4.   **Fear is the root of all failures.**

I heard God speak to me in my spirit that fear is the root of all our failures! Yes, "all" our failures. Fear is the reason we fail in any area of our lives.

Fear is the root of all failures even in the lives of the unsaved world. Even though we understand that the unsaved world is being ruled by Satan, he really does not have as much right and power as we sometimes think he has. If Satan had unlimited power, he would have killed us in our sins to prevent us from coming to Jesus.

In fact, if Satan had his way with everyone, he would have killed all of us before we were born. He is killing a lot of babies today in their mothers' wombs. You or I could have been one of them. Abortion is killing millions of innocent babies.

Think about the devilish procedure in America called partial-birth abortion. Babies that are almost full term (and sometimes full term) are literally murdered before their whole body comes out of the mother's womb. Some devil-possessed and twisted minds think that if the full body does not come out, then that is not a live human being. Those babies have no way of defending themselves. Most of us in the world sit back and watch these poor babies murdered.

I want you to know today that the devil is a killer. He has twisted the minds of the world to think that a baby is not a baby until he or she comes out of the womb. How did the devil get the path or permission to commit all these murders? I can show you that it is through fear. Do you know why we have used the pronoun "it" for babies all through the ages? It is because in the past, we did not have any sonograms to enable us determine the sex of babies. We didn't know whether to call them boys or girls. So we settled on the pronoun "it." Today, we are able to determine very early whether the baby is a boy or girl. So we should change our pronoun. Referring to an unborn baby as an "it", de-humanizes the baby. We should refer to an unborn baby as "he" or "she."

5.   **Acting on fear is acting on the word of the devil.**

You wouldn't be afraid if the devil had not planted a seed of fear in your mind. The devil said something to you that made you afraid. God's Word will never put fear in us. God's Word can

The Nature of Fear

only put faith in us. Acting in faith is acting on God's Word. Conversely, acting in fear is acting on the Word of the devil.

Chapter 4

Fear First Expressed In The Bible

Let us go back to the Book of Beginnings. We learned that there was no fear in Adam and Eve until they disobeyed God. They obeyed another voice instead of the voice of God. Fear has a voice and faith has a voice. The voice of faith is the voice of God. The voice of fear is the voice of the devil. Anytime God speaks to you through His Word, He intends for your faith to be increased. God's Word should never produce fear. It should produce only faith. Anytime Satan speaks to you, he intends for your fear to be increased.

> *"Now the serpent was more subtle than any beast of the field which the LORD God had made. And he said unto the woman, Yea, hath God said, Ye shall not eat of every tree of the garden?"*
> *(Genesis 3:1)*

Most of our problems in life start with questions. Most of our doubts begin when we question God's Word.

Satan began to put doubt into Eve's mind asking the question, "Did God really say?" God does not need the devil to interpret the Bible to us. God has placed the Holy Spirit within us to interpret His Word to us. If you are not very firm in your knowledge of the Word of God, you can be easily fooled by Satan when he brings questions

13

into your mind. My advice to you is that if God has said it in His Word, then you simply need to believe it. You simply need to act on it. You don't need to ask questions. Remember that your questions are the beginning of doorways to the devil to come in and do damage to your life.

The devil will bring negative thoughts and questions to your mind. What do you do with those thoughts? Don't take the thoughts. The Bible teaches that the way we take thoughts is by speaking them out of our mouths *(Matthew 6:31)*. When negative thoughts and questions come to your mind, replace them by the Word of God. Focus on what God has said in His Word. Meditating on God's Word will drive off Satan's thoughts and questions.

If Satan had free access to Adam and Eve, he would simply have used that path. But he had to seek a path through questions and doubts which result in fear. The devil uses the same tactics today to gain a path into our lives. He cannot just get into our lives simply because he wants to. We must grant him access.

Faith does not ask questions. Fear does. Faith makes declarations. Some of us have been asking too many questions in our lives. We need to make more declarations. How do you make declarations? You get into God's Word until the Word takes root in your heart. Then you begin to say what God's Word says about you.

Satan cannot do any harm in our lives unless we let him. The Bible says we should not give any place to the devil. That means we are the ones who give place to the devil. If the devil had total freedom, he would have done more damage to this world than he has done. He will do only what we allow him to do. Compare this fact with the concept of electricity.

The electric poles outside our buildings may carry as much as seven hundred and twenty volts of electricity. There may be a lot of electric power in them, ready to provide light to our home. But if we do not have the right electric wiring in our home, we cannot receive that electricity. Faith and fear are conductors of power. Faith is the conductor that brings the power of God into our lives. Conversely, fear is the wiring and the conductor that allows the power of the devil to be brought into our lives. Without fear, the devil cannot do what he plans to do in our lives.

Sometimes, we as Christians have the wrong idea that nothing will happen to us unless it is God's will. Can you look at all the terrible things happening in the world today and tell me all of that is God's will? Do you think God just decided that terrorists should blow up America's World Trade Center on Nine-Eleven? Do you think it is God's will for babies to be dying in poor countries from starvation? What about all the other disasters occurring in the world? Can you say all that is God's will? No, God is not responsible for any of that. If it was all God's will, then that would make Him a pretty evil God. No,

God is not both good and bad. He is only good. He gives only good and perfect gifts.

You may still be asking why all these terrible things are happening in the world. The Bible has answers to all your questions. But when you start asking questions instead of simply believing God's Word, then you are acting in fear and not faith. Faith is absolute trust in God.

Please go back with me to Genesis:

"And the woman said unto the serpent, We may eat of the fruit of the trees of the garden: But of the fruit of the tree which is in the midst of the garden, God hath said, Ye shall not eat of it, neither shall ye touch it, lest ye die" **(Genesis 3:2-3).**

Do you see what is happening here? The woman starts to have conversation with the devil. Any time you start having conversation with the devil, you must look out for danger. If you don't know the difference between the voice of God and that of the devil, then you better get back into the Bible and begin sowing the Word into your heart.

Did you notice that Eve added something new to God's instruction? God only said they should not "eat", but He never said they couldn't "touch" it. We often do the same thing today. We add to God's Word and twist it. We sometimes take things away from the Word to make the Word say what we want to hear. Instead of going to the Bible and checking things out for ourselves, we often just assume that everything

16

we hear from another Christian (even preachers) is entirely correct.

> *"And the serpent said to the woman, Ye shall not surely die. For God knows that in the day ye eat thereof, then your eyes shall be opened, and ye shall be as gods, knowing good and evil"* **(Genesis 3:4-5).**

Why on earth do we need the devil to start interpreting God's Word to us? The devil will only twist the Word of God to us. Satan told Eve that if they ate of the forbidden fruit, their eyes would be opened and they would be "as gods." Adam and Eve were already "as gods."

> *"And when the woman saw that the tree was good for food, and that it was pleasant to the eyes, and a tree to be desired to make one wise, she took of the fruit thereof, and did eat, and gave also unto her husband with her; and he did eat"* **(Genesis 3:6).**

What started her fall? A question! Where do you start your downfall? Where do you start your decline? Where do you start giving a path to the devil in your life? You start with a question! Eve started with a question. Then she went on to engage the devil in a conversation and the devil was attempting to interpret the Word of God to her. The only talking you need to do to the devil is to tell him to "Shut Up!" As a child of God, you have authority to command Satan to get out of your life. Tell him you don't listen to any spirit but God's Spirit. Tell him "It is written!"

Listening to the devil caused Eve to disobey God's commandment. The Word states that she was deceived but the man was not. Adam should have taken responsibility as the head of this union and covered his wife. The whole outcome of this event could have been different. If men today would learn to cover their wives instead of blaming them, things would be better. Instead of doing what was right, Adam entered into transgression with his wife.

> *"And the eyes of them both were opened, and they knew that they were naked; and they sewed fig leaves together, and made themselves aprons"* **(Genesis 3:7).**

The devil did say that their eyes would be opened. But that was only a partial truth. The devil often deceives Christians by mixing his lies with a little portion of the truth from the Word of God. The devil said their eyes would be opened and they would become like gods. But notice what happened; their eyes were opened and they knew they were naked.

Adam and Even didn't know they were naked until they disobeyed God. Satan tricked them to disobey God's command. Disobedience brings shame.

> *"And they heard the voice of the LORD God walking in the garden in the cool of the day: and Adam and his wife hid themselves from the presence of the LORD God amongst the trees of the garden"* **(Genesis 3:8).**

Fear First Expressed In The Bible

God came down to the garden every day and had fellowship with Adam and Eve. Scripture does not tell us how long God and Adam and Eve shared fellowship together in the garden before the fall. It could have been a very long time. Adam and Eve had close fellowship with God. They were never afraid of Him. But this time, they hid themselves when they heard the voice of God as He was coming down to them. They hid themselves among the trees of the garden.

It is interesting that we sometimes think we can hide from God. God is omnipresent. He is everywhere at the same time. He sees everything. So if you've done something wrong, don't run from God. If the devil has deceived you and led you into sin, don't think you can hide from God. Run to God! Even when you think you have messed up, you still need to run to God because God is our refuge.

> "God is our refuge and strength, a very present help in trouble" **(Psalm 46:1)**.

> "And the LORD God called unto Adam, and said unto him, Where art thou? And he said, I heard thy voice in the garden, and I was afraid, because I was naked; and I hid myself" **(Genesis 3:9-10)**.

God knew where Adam and Eve were but still asked them where they were. Adam's response was the first time the expression of fear was ever recorded. That was the time negative fear entered into the world.

FREEDOM FROM FEAR

When fear was first expressed in the garden, it was the result of disobedience. The disobedience of Adam and Eve brought fear. They obeyed the serpent instead of obeying God. Instead of acting on the Word of God, they acted on the word of the serpent. Their disobedience caused them to have fear.

From that time onwards, fear became the tool that Satan uses to cause people to disobey God. In the garden, disobedience led to fear. Today, fear leads to disobedience. Fear causes us not to listen to God's Word. The fear of failure causes us not to trust God's Word. The fear of lack causes us not to obey God's Word regarding giving. We are afraid that if we gave generously, we might run out of resources.

After having fellowship with God over a period of time, Adam and Eve must have known that God was trustworthy. But they still disobeyed. When God says something in His Word, we can be sure that it will be just as He said it would be. But Satan sows fear in our minds to cause us to disobey God's Word. People in the world are ruled by Satan all their lifetime because of fear. People are tormented by fear because fear has torment *(1 John 4:18)*.

Chapter 5

Examples of Fearlessness

If you do not have any fear, then the devil, who comes to you, cannot do to you what he has come to do. The absence of fear makes it impossible for the devil to do anything to you. Philippians 1:28 says that your fearlessness is the evidence of your salvation. This is what saves you from the attack of the devil. Your fearlessness is the seal and proof that the devil cannot do what he has come to do – which is to steal, kill and destroy your life.

Example of Shadrach, Meshach and Abednego

The three Hebrew boys, Shadrach, Meshach and Abednego, in the Book of Daniel, were not afraid of King Nebuchadnezzar. This story is one of the greatest illustrations of fearlessness. Even though the king threatened to put them into the fiery furnace, they did not allow fear to overcome them. The Hebrew boys had no fear. Fear doesn't talk back to a king. If they had fear, they would have bowed. Here's my own translation of what they said to the king, *"O King, we don't even care to answer you in this matter. If you put us in the fire, the God whom we serve is able to get us out of the fire. But even if you do not put us in the fire, we want you to know that we are not going to serve your gods or worship your dumb golden image."* Read it for yourself in the book of Daniel.

"Shadrach, Meshach and Abednego answered and said to the king, O Nebuchadnezzar, we are not careful to answer thee in this matter. If it be so, our God whom we serve is able to deliver us from the burning fiery furnace, and he will deliver us out of thine hand, O king. But if not [if you do not put us into the fire], *be it known unto thee, O king, that we will not serve thy gods, nor worship the golden image which thou hast set up" **(Daniel 3: 16-18).***

The king told them; "if you bow, you won't burn." The Hebrew boys said; "No King, you got it wrong, if we bow, we will burn. If we don't bow, we won't burn." They did not bow, and they did not burn. The king put them in the fire, but they did not burn. They did not even smell of smoke.

Sometimes people come up with foolish explanations to discredit miracles recorded in the Bible. You might have heard the popular explanation that the children of Israel were able to walk through the Red Sea just because the water was only ankle-deep. Yes, indeed, if the water was only ankle-deep, then that was an even greater miracle because the whole Egyptian army drowned in ankle-deep water.

Some people might think that the furnace wasn't really that hot. Don't let anyone deceive you about the temperature of the furnace. The Bible said it was a "fiery" furnace. It was very hot. It was so hot that the flame at the entrance of the furnace killed the mighty men who threw the Hebrew boys into the furnace.

Just like the Hebrew boys, if we do not have fear, there is nothing that the devil can do to us. He may bring his attacks. He may even put us into the fiery furnaces of life. But our Covenant God will deliver us if we do not fear. Remember that Philippians 1:28 says your fearlessness is the evidence of your deliverance.

We need to know that God does not always deliver us "from" things. Sometimes, He delivers us "in the midst" of the circumstances. We may be thrown in the fiery furnaces of life sometimes. But God comes in there with us and protects us from burning. We may walk through the valley of the shadow of death; but we shall fear no evil because God will be with us.

Example of David

Even though the devil may plan an attack against you, it doesn't mean that he can get to you. The fact that you are attacked does not mean you have been overcome. The devil may only be tempting you with some symptoms to see if you will give in to fear. He is waiting for you to give him an inroad into your life. If you don't allow fear, the devil can't get to you. When you are faced with challenges, it is important to remember the past victories that God has given you.

23

> *"And David said unto Saul, Thy servant kept his father's sheep, and there came a lion, and a bear, and took a lamb out of the flock: And I went out after him, and smote him, and delivered it out of his mouth: and when he arose against me, I caught him by his beard, and smote him, and slew him. Thy servant slew both the lion and the bear: and this uncircumcised Philistine shall be as one of them, seeing he hath defied the armies of the living God. David said moreover, The LORD that delivered me out of the paw of the lion, and out of the paw of the bear, he will deliver me out of the hand of this Philistine......."* **(I Samuel 17: 34-37).**

David killed a lion and a bear, not a dog and a cat. A lion and a bear, two of the most feared beasts of the field. David had no fear in him. He did not say; "Oh, it's only one lamb." When the enemy comes against us in any area of our lives, we should not say, "Well, that's only a small area." No, he will take up more territory if we just sit back and allow him. Do you know why David did not compromise with the lion and the bear? It is because he was not afraid. He would not have run after the lion and the bear if he was afraid. If it was some of us, we might have said to ourselves; "I'm not going to mess with a lion. I'm not going to mess with a bear. That lion can help himself. That bear can help himself. I will just tell Daddy that we lost one lamb today. Daddy will understand that it was a lion. Daddy will understand that it was a bear."

Examples of Fearlessness

When the lion rose against David, David caught the lion by its beard and killed it. Does that sound like the work of someone who is afraid? Not at all! David was just a young man. He wasn't even a giant. We know he was small in stature because later on, he tried on King Saul's armor and it was too big for him. David might have been small on the outside, but he was very big on the inside. Without fear, you can conquer anything. Without fear, you can overcome any obstacle the devil puts in your way. It doesn't matter what you are facing today. Without fear, you can conquer that problem.

David ran towards Goliath, the Philistine giant, in the same way that he ran towards the lion and the bear. When you don't have fear, you will not run away from your problems. Without fear, you will run towards your problems. Your problem may roar at you like an old lion. But, without fear, you will run to the roar.

When you focus on the problem and fear grips your heart, that fear only magnifies the problem. You need to remember that when Satan first shows up at your door step, it is only a bluff. He is only checking us out to see how much you know and how much faith you have. You need to "call his bluff." He is like an old toothless lion. He cannot hurt you. The Bible says, *"Be sober, be vigilant, because your adversary the devil, as a roaring lion walketh about, seeking whom he may devour"* **(1 Peter 5:8).** Do you know what the old lion does? The old lion roars very loud just to scare the prey and cause the prey to run. The younger and stronger lions hide behind the prey, knowing that the prey will run away from the roar and run into their trap. But if you run to the roar, like David did towards Goliath, the old lion cannot hurt you. It is toothless.

Is the God of David any different from the God of today? Is He not the same God? Did He not promise that He will be with us always? Yes, He is with us. But even more than that, He is in us. Why then should we be afraid? We need to be God-conscious! We need to be God-inside minded! We should not allow fear to make us think that God will not make it on time. God is always on time!

The Word of power is in our mouth. All we need to do is act with the same amount of faith as David did. It will happen for us in the same way that it happened for David. We must be of good courage. We must *only be not afraid.* It will happen for us in the same way that it happened for Joshua. God is no respecter of persons. He sees you in the same way as He saw David and Joshua.

It doesn't matter how big your giant is today. It doesn't matter how big your problem seems to you. Only be not afraid. We should not measure how big our problems are. We should measure how big our God is. We have a BIG GOD. He is bigger than any circumstance we might face today. The children of Israel were focusing on how big the Philistine giants were instead of focusing on how big their God was. How big is your God, to you, today? Is He El-Shaddai to you? Is He the God who is more than enough for you?

I am not teaching you to deny that you have problems. Some religions teach you to ignore the problem. They want you to say; "Tata, there is no such thing as sickness. There is no such thing as evil. It's not real. It's all in your imagination. Just imagine that the problem doesn't exist, and it will go away!" No, no, no, no, that's not what I'm teaching.

The devil is real. Sickness is real. Poverty is real. Yes, fear is real. But I am encouraging you to focus more on God than on fear. God is bigger than your problems. And that BIG GOD lives on the inside of you. So, in fact, you are bigger than your problems. The devil does not have a right over you; because of what Jesus did at Calvary. Jesus whipped him. Instead of you being afraid, you should put on your Jesus armor. That will make the devil the one who fears because he recognizes that Jesus armor you are wearing. He remembers how badly Jesus defeated him in hell.

It is our responsibility to stand our ground against the devil. The only way we can do this is by not having any fear. Let us turn to Psalm 23 and see what David wrote. If anyone knows anything about faith and courage, it must be David. If there was one man who did not have any fear, it must be David. This was the David who ran after the lion, the bear and after Goliath.

"The LORD is my shepherd; I shall not want. He makes me to lie down in green pastures; He leads me beside the still waters. He restores my soul; He leads me in the paths of righteousness For His name's sake. Yea, though I walk through the valley of the shadow of death, I will fear no evil; For You are with me; Your rod and Your staff, they comfort me. You prepare a table before me in the presence of my enemies; You anoint my head with oil; My cup runs over. Surely goodness and mercy shall follow me all the days of my life; And I will dwell in the house of the LORD Forever" **(Psalm 23)**.

Are you able to say today, without fear, that the LORD is your Shepherd? If the LORD is your Shepherd, can you, by faith, say you have everything that you need? Do you know what real prosperity is? Prosperity is not just having a lot of money. David is saying here that he does not have any lack. Whatever he needs is always there. Why? Because the LORD is his Shepherd!

David continued and said; *"He makes me lie down in green pastures."* Green! Green, like the color of money. Can you join me today in declaring like David? "I will never have any lack or want in my life, because I am following the Shepherd of my life. Jesus is my Shepherd. He is always making me lie down in green pastures. Therefore, I will have no lack or want." Think about this! When does a cow lie down in green pastures? Only after it has eaten and gets full.

And if that wasn't enough, David said; *"He leads me beside the still waters."* This signifies a place of peace. David said that even when he is close to death, he will fear no evil. When someone walks through the valley of the shadow of death, it means that person is very close to death. There is no telling how many times you and I might have been very close to death without realizing it. We should have no fear even if we know we are close to death. Why? God is with us. Why should I be afraid when God is with me? When you have this type of attitude of fearlessness, you will not die even if you're close to death.

Shadrach, Meshach and Abednego feared no evil because they knew God was with them. Who did the king see when he looked in the fire? He saw a fourth man in the fire. He said he saw someone like the Son of God! God was in the fire with them.

Let us look at another example of David in Psalm 27:

"The LORD is my light and my salvation; Whom shall I fear? The LORD is the strength of my life; Of whom shall I be afraid?" **(Psalm 27:1)**

Can you say the LORD is your light today? Note carefully that the LORD is not just light. He is your light. Why then would you stumble? As long as the LORD, your Light, is shining around you and inside you, you should not stumble. David didn't only say the LORD was his light. He said the LORD was his salvation. That means deliverance. That means that if anything came close to him, the LORD would take care of it.

David continued and said the LORD is the strength of his life. Is the LORD the strength of your life today? Or are you depending on your own strength? Can you be like David and say; *"Of whom shall I be afraid?"* It is very obvious that David knew something special about God. There was something that kept fear from getting inside David right from his youth. David recognized that God was with him. Look at what he says in the next two verses:

> *"When the wicked came against me to eat up my flesh, My enemies and foes, They stumbled and fell. Though an army may encamp against me, My heart shall not fear; Though war may rise against me, In this I will be confident"* **(Psalm 27: 2-3).**

Notice that David did not deny that he had enemies and problems. He knew that they were there. He knew that the devil had a host of demons which caused people to rise up against him. But he said his heart would not fear. As a believer, you will still have problems. The devil will still bring tests and trials into your life. You will still have circumstances that will try to produce fear in you.

Like David, you must be able to say that even when the wicked, your enemies and your foes come to eat up your flesh, they will stumble and fall. Isn't that better than you stumbling and falling and being eaten up? How funny do you think the Bible story would have been if David stumbled and fell while running after the lion and the bear? How sad would that have been if he got eaten up? But we see many Christians stumbling and falling and being eaten up by the devil.

Remember again that the absence of fear is the evident token of your enemy's destruction. It is the evidence of your deliverance. *(Philippians 1:28)*. Whatever the devil may have brought against you today; whether it is against your mind, your physical body or against your property, he cannot be successful if you do not have fear. Without fear, there is no path for him to get through to you. He has no access to your life.

Chapter 6

God Knows How To Deliver You

Regardless of what the devil has brought against you, if you act in faith and trust in God, God knows how to deliver you. Do you remember what David said?

"Yea, though I walk through the valley of the shadow of death, I will fear no evil; For You are with me..." **(Ps. 23:4)**

When you are at death's door, you don't need to be afraid. If you're afraid, you will die. In such critical moments, you need to let your faith rise up in you.

You may have heard the story some years ago of two 747 airplanes that crashed on the runway. There was a very heavy fog that day. Several airplanes had to wait their turn on the runway. One of the pilots was very impatient. He got tired of waiting. He did not pay attention to the instruction of the air-controllers. He felt that he could see the way clear. So, instead of waiting, he decided to go. He revved up the engine and began to take off.

What he did not know or see was that another 747 was just taxiing on the same runway that he was taking off on. By the time the impatient pilot saw the other 747, it was too late. He did not have sufficient power to pull up the airplane. He cut right into the other 747. Several hundreds of people were burned to death including the impatient pilot.

In the midst of that calamity, there were some good stories. One of those stories was told by one of the passengers who had no fear. He was a very overweight person and therefore could not move fast. When the crash occurred, the first thing out of his mouth was "In the Name of JESUS!"

On the contrary, when they found and reviewed the airplane's black box, what they heard was very sad. They heard the first word that came out of the mouth of that impatient pilot when the planes crashed. He said "God Damned!" What a sad statement to make just before departing to eternity!

I suspect you have heard that unfortunate statement several times. Do you know what is wrong with that statement? God is not "Damned." God does not damn anything or anyone. The devil is the one who damns and destroys, but not God. Have you ever heard anyone say "Buddha Damned?" or "Mohamed Damned?" Why do people always say "God Damned?"

We need to be careful what we say with our mouth when we are in the middle of crises. The overweight brother called upon the name of the Savior, Jesus! The man was so close to the inferno of the burning plane that he literally saw people's skins melt off in the fire.

God Knows How To Deliver You

He said he suddenly looked up and there was a hole in the ceiling of the airplane. Upon shouting the name of JESUS, he found himself holding on to the top of that hole in the top of the airplane. His upper body was sticking out of the airplane. He said there was no way he could have lifted himself that high because of his excessive weight. He didn't know how he got there. The only thing he remembered was shouting the name of JESUS.

As he continued shouting the name of JESUS, he found himself on top of the plane, near a wing. He decided to slide down the wing of the airplane. The engines of the plane were still roaring. He could easily have been sucked into the engine. Even though the wings were very high up from the ground, he had faith that God would take care of him if he jumped. He jumped and landed safely, crawled away from the burning airplane and was safe.

Listen, my friend! It does not matter how dark it looks around you today. It does not matter how grave the situation around you seems. God knows how to deliver you. You must act in faith, with trust and confidence in God that He is with you. You must not act in fear or speak fear-filled words. God knows how to deliver you and He will deliver you.

Chapter 7

God Is Our Refuge

David had a special faith connection with God. That was why he said,

"Yea, though I walk through the valley of the shadow of death, I will fear no evil; For You are with me..." **(Ps. 23:4)**

We all need to work on our connection with God. We need to work on our fellowship with God. This will enable us to have faith in God in the midst of tests and trials. The right words will come out of our mouths. We will talk and act like David. There will be no fear in our hearts. We will trust in God and know that He is with us. He is for us. He is in us. He is on our side. When we feel lonely and abandoned, we will remember that He said God will never leave us nor forsake us.

Let us look at another one of David's faith confessions:

"God is our refuge and strength, A very present help in trouble. Therefore we will not fear, Even though the earth be removed, And though the mountains be carried into the midst of the sea; Though its waters roar and be troubled, Though the mountains shake with its swelling. Selah! There is a river whose streams shall make glad the city of God, The holy place of the tabernacle of the Most High.

37

God is in the midst of her, she shall not be moved; God shall help her, just at the break of dawn. The nations raged, the kingdoms were moved; He uttered His voice, the earth melted. The LORD of hosts is with us; The God of Jacob is our refuge. Selah" **(Psalm 46: 1-7).**

God does not take a vacation when you get into trouble. He will be right there with you in the trouble. In the time of trouble, God will hide you in a secret place where the devil cannot find you.

"For in the time of trouble He shall hide me in His pavilion: in the secret of His tabernacle shall He hide me; He shall set me up upon a rock" **(Psalm 27:5).**

When a hunter is going after an animal, as soon as that animal enters a game reserve or a wild life refuge, that animal is safe. The hunter cannot kill the animal in the place of refuge. But if the animal leaves the reserve, then it is fair game. Satan cannot come near you when you are in God's pavilion.

Shadrach, Meshach and Abednego knew that God would be with them in trouble. David knew that God was with him. God was his refuge and strength, a very present help in trouble. Therefore he would not fear. David demonstrated throughout his life that he had no fear.

Are you able to say today that you will not be afraid if someone suddenly pulls the rug from under your feet? What will you do when the earth from under you seems to be removed? Could you be like David? David did not just pay lip service. He talked the talk and walked the walk. He backed his talk with actions. Will you be able to do that?

What would you do if the *"waters roar and be troubled?"* What would you do in the middle of a hurricane or tornado? Will you allow fear to overcome you? Or will you be like David and not be afraid? There was a story on the *700 Club* about a woman and her son. They were caught in the middle of a powerful tornado while driving. Before she knew it, her vehicle was lifted up by the tornado as high as the top of a light pole. The wheels of the vehicle were still turning while the car was in the air.

The vehicle was slammed back on the ground and she fell to the floor of the vehicle. She said all she new was that a scripture popped up in her mouth. She did not know a whole lot about the Word of God. But she remembered a very simple scripture. All scripture is powerful, no matter how simple they may seem.

While she lay down and covered her child, she heard a voice tell her to reach out and put the vehicle into parking gear. When the vehicle came back down, it landed just a few yards in front of a house. If she had not listened to that voice and put the vehicle in park, it would have run straight into the house. There is no telling what damage would have been caused.

Thank God, there was not even a scratch on the mother and her child. Who protected her? That is the God we serve! That is the LORD Jehovah. The I AM! Our El-Shaddai – the God who is more than enough! Jesus is our LORD. Jesus is our SAVIOR. He is our DELIVERER! Hallelujah! Like David, I can say; God is on my side! God is my deliverer! God is my fortress. God is my refuge. Why do I need to be afraid?

Let us look at one more Psalm of David:

"Be merciful to me, O God, for man would swallow me up; Fighting all day he oppresses me. My enemies would hound me all day, For there are many who fight against me, O Most High. Whenever I am afraid, I will trust in You. In God (I will praise His word), In God I have put my trust; I will not fear. What can flesh do to me?" **(Psalm 56: 1-4).**

Have you ever felt daily oppressions from people? Does it seem sometimes like your enemies want to swallow you up? Do you sometimes feel like you have many enemies all coming against you at the same time? Notice what David says in verse 3. He said; *"whenever I am afraid, I will trust in you."* David did not deny his fear. He simply denied the right of fear to get in him. Instead of fear, what are we going to do? Trust Him! Trust who? Trust our God! Like David, we will praise God's Word. We will put one hundred percent of our trust in Him and not be afraid. We will not fear what flesh can do to us.

God Is Our Refuge

Let us read some more of Psalm 56:

"When I cry out to You, Then my enemies will turn back; This I know, because God is for me. In God (I will praise His word), In the LORD (I will praise His word), In God I have put my trust; I will not be afraid. What can man do to me?"
(Psalm 56: 9-11).

When I cry unto the LORD, what happens to my enemies? They will turn back. David said; *"This I know."* Why did David know his enemies would turn back? He said; *"This I know, because God is for me."* Do you know that God is for you? Do you think God was more for David than He is for you? In fact, God is more for you today than He was for David because God lives inside you. God did not make His home inside of David. David lived under the Old Covenant. You and I live under a new and better Covenant with better promises. God has come to dwell inside you. You should be able to trust Him at least as much as David did.

If you know God is in you, you should be able to praise His Word. The Word of God has everything to do with your victory. Let us all be bold and say; *"In God have I put my trust."* "IN GOD WE TRUST" should not only be written on our dollar bills. It should be written in our hearts. If we truly trust in God, we will not be afraid of anything. Instead of fear, we will have faith. We will live in victory. The devil cannot harm us.

Even if the devil comes to put some sickness or disease in your body, if you do not fear, he cannot harm you. People often become fear-stricken at the mention of some diseases. Diseases like "cancer." Just the mention of that name "cancer," puts fear in people.

I heard a very well known preacher give his testimony of what fear can do to us. He said while he was bathing, he noticed that there was a bump on his chest that had not been there before. His mind started to wonder what that lump might be. He found himself pinching that bump frequently until it started to really hurt.

His mind went back to what he had heard in the past. He had heard that a hard bump was bad, but a soft bump might not be too bad. We need to realize that the devil plants seeds of fear in our hearts. When a situation like that bump comes up, then that seed of fear begins to grow. What that preacher heard in the past about hard and soft bumps was a seed of fear.

He complained to his wife about how the bump was hurting. The wife said, "Keep your hands off it. The reason it's hurting you so much is that you have been squeezing and mashing that bump every day." The man asked his wife what he should do. The wife suggested he should go and see a doctor. He was afraid of what the doctor might diagnose.

He finally agreed and went to see a doctor. After the doctor examined him, the doctor said; "I think we need to take a biopsy of this bump." Biopsy is the process of removing a sample tissue for further examination. After the biopsy, the doctor came back to the room with a surprised look on his face. The doctor said; "O, My, I have never seen anything like this before." Then the doctor got up and walked out of the room.

You can imagine what must have been going through the preacher's mind. He was probably thinking he was going to die the next day. Fear was rising up in his heart. The doctor came back and explained what he was shocked about. The doctor said he had never seen such a simple and harmless fatty tissue like that before. It was merely fat that had accumulated and turned into a little bump. But you can imagine the fear and torment that the preacher must have gone through.

We all have opportunities to become afraid. If we are not careful, we will allow the enemy to get into our affairs by allowing fear in our hearts. Instead of fear, we need to let the devil know that we have faith in God. We need to let Satan know that he cannot succeed in his attempts to harm us. We need to be speaking the words of Psalm 91 every day.

"He that dwelleth in the secret place of the most High shall abide under the shadow of the Almighty" **(Psalm 91:1).**

Every morning when we get up, we should declare that we are dwelling in God's secret place.

We should declare that God is our refuge, our fortress, our hiding place and we should put all our trust in Him. It must be a good feeling to know that God's shadow is over us all the time.

If we are truly honest with ourselves, we would admit that we ought to dwell in God's secret place all the time. We were bought with a price. We belong to God. We should not live just any way and anywhere we want to live. In honor and appreciation to the one who purchased us with His precious blood, we should dedicate our lives to Him. We should have constant fellowship with Him. He enjoys fellowship with us. There is no other place more peaceful than with God. There is no other place more enjoyable than with God. There is no other place safer than with God.

God doesn't want you to check in with Him only once in a while. He is not a cheap motel or hotel room. He wants you to dwell in Him and He wants to dwell in you. Do you remember Jesus' Words in John Chapter 15 and also His prayer in Chapter 17?

> "Abide in me, and I in you. As the branch cannot bear fruit of itself, except it abide in the vine; no more can ye, except ye abide in me" **(John 15:4).**

> "I pray for them: I pray not for the world, but for them which thou hast given me; for they are thine. And all mine are thine, and thine are mine; and I am glorified in them" **(John 17: 9-10).**

God Is Our Refuge

"That they all may be one; as thou, Father, art in me, and I in thee, that they also may be one in us: that the world may believe that thou hast sent me. And the glory which thou gavest me I have given them; that they may be one, even as we are one: I in them, and thou in me, that they may be made perfect in one; and that the world may know that thou hast sent me, and hast loved them, as thou hast loved me" **(John 17: 21-23).**

God wants us to dwell in His secret place. I believe that this secret place is the Word of God. It is both the Written Word and the Living Word. The Living Word is resident in our hearts and in our mouths. It is important for us to feed on the Word of God on a regular basis so our minds will continue to be renewed and our hearts refreshed. If you live in the Word and the Word lives in you, Jesus said in John 15:7 that you can ask anything you want and it will be done for you.

Chapter 8

Speak Words of Faith

If you live (abide) in the Word (the secret place), then you will always be under the shadow of the Almighty. Notice in Psalm 91, verse 2 that if you dwell in God's secret place, you will "say" something. It is very important what you say with your mouth. It is important what you say about yourself.

"I will say of the LORD, He is my refuge and my fortress: my God; in him will I trust" (Psalm 91:2).

It doesn't matter what the devil brings against me. I know that my God will deliver me. The LORD is my refuge. The LORD is my fortress. My job is to remain in the "Secret Place." The secret place is the Word of God. I should live and breathe and feed on the Word of God. I should always recognize that it is in Him that I live and move and have my being. My heart and my mouth should be filled with the Word of God. His Word should not depart out of my mouth. I should meditate therein day and night.

When I face challenges and danger, the first words out of my mouth should be; "The LORD is my Shepherd. The LORD is my Refuge. He is my Shield. He is my Buckler. He is my Fortress. He is my Deliverer. He is my High Tower. He is everything to me." The person who dwells in God's secret place will never say he is afraid.

Our faith and trust in God should be one hundred percent. You cannot trust God half way and be half way afraid. When you are faced with trouble, you must decide which side you are on. You cannot say God is your refuge and still be afraid. Do not be like the squirrel in the middle of the road. The squirrel doesn't seem to know which direction to go. It vacillates, going one way, stops, and turns the other way. Do you know where the squirrel ends up? It ends up dead – run over by the car! Don't get killed by the devil because of your indecision.

Another important reminder for us is that we should stay in fellowship with other believers. If you watch the Discovery Channel on TV, you will notice that when carnivorous animals are hunting their prey, they focus on one that is astray from the pack. When tigers and lions are stalking deer, they never attack the whole pack. They try to isolate and steer one away from the pack and attack that one. They often look for an animal that is weak.

Don't allow yourself to become weak. Stay strong and stay with the pack of believers. The devil will not affect you when you stay under the wings of the Almighty. Look at the next two verses:

> "Surely he shall deliver thee from the snare of the fowler, and from the noisome pestilence. He shall cover thee with his

feathers, and under his wings shalt thou trust: his truth shall be thy shield and buckler" (Psalm 91: 3-4).

When you are under God's wings, you will not be afraid. When God has put you in His pavilion, there is no room for fear. Say out loud to yourself and to the devil, "No fear here!"

Let us read the rest of Psalm 91 and see what happens to the person who dwells in God's secret place.

"Thou shalt not be afraid for the terror by night; nor for the arrow that flieth by day; Nor for the pestilence that walketh in darkness; nor for the destruction that wasteth at noonday. A thousand shall fall at thy side, and ten thousand at thy right hand; but it shall not come nigh thee"
(Psalm 91: 5-7).

If there was some disaster and you saw one thousand people fall dead at your side, would you not be tempted to fear? What about ten thousand? All of them dead and you are the only one standing. This scripture says if you don't have any fear, a thousand could fall at your side and ten thousand at your right hand, but you will still be standing. If you believe that the Word of God is real, then you should believe that this could happen for you. We live in very dangerous times in the world today. If there is any time that we should trust God for His protection, it must be now.

FREEDOM FROM FEAR

When God was bringing the Jews out of Egypt, they were right in the middle of all the plagues and destruction that were happening to the Egyptians. But none of the Jews were affected.

The LORD is my refuge. I am not trusting in what man can do for me or against me. I am not even trusting in our great nation of the United States. I thank God for the United States of America. I thank God for the Army, the Navy, the Air-Force and the Marines. I thank God for their protection. But I am trusting only in God for my deliverance in time of trouble. We should honor and support our service men for their sacrifice. We should thank God for them. But I do not put my trust in them. I put my trust only in God Almighty.

See the promises of protection in the remaining verses of Psalm 91 below:

> "Only with thine eyes shalt thou behold and see the reward of the wicked. Because thou hast made the LORD, which is my refuge, even the most High, thy habitation; There shall no evil befall thee, neither shall any plague come nigh thy dwelling. For he shall give his angels charge over thee, to keep thee in all thy ways. They shall bear thee up in their hands, lest thou dash thy foot against a stone. Thou shalt tread upon the lion and adder: the young lion and the dragon shalt thou trample under feet. Because he hath set his love upon me, therefore will I

deliver him: I will set him on high, because he hath known my name. He shall call upon me, and I will answer him: I will be with him in trouble; I will deliver him, and honour him. With long life will I satisfy him, and show him my salvation" **(Psalm 91: 8-16).**

David again said *"The LORD is on my side; I will not fear: what can man do unto me?"* **(Psalm 118:6).** How do we have the ability not to be afraid? We must know that the LORD is on our side. If you want to live without fear, then you must know that God is on your side. But it goes even further than that. The revelation for the church today is no longer that God is on our side. God is inside us.

The Bible is full of references to living without fear. Let us look at the book of Isaiah.

"Fear thou not; for I am with thee: be not dismayed; for I am thy God: I will strengthen thee; yea, I will help thee; yea, I will uphold thee with the right hand of my righteousness" **(Isaiah 41:10).**

God has given us His own Word that He is with us. If we are afraid, then it means we do not believe God's Word. All that God wants us to do is to keep fear out and not be dismayed. He says He will do the rest. What a bargain! The word "dismayed" is defined in the dictionary as "the pressure of sudden fear." This is when it feels like fear suddenly swoops down on us like a hawk on a small bird. Another word for dismay is

51

"anxiety." The Bible tells us in Philippians 4:6 not to be anxious about anything. Anxiety is sudden fear.

Sometimes, fear disguises itself as worry. You might say you do not have fear, but do you worry sometimes? Worrying is a form of fear. Worrying is a slander on God's promises. You might be asking yourself, "Everybody worries sometimes don't they?" We all have the opportunity to worry, but we don't have to give in to it. We all have the opportunity to be afraid, but we don't have to seize that opportunity.

How is it possible to live a life free of anxiety? God says He will strengthen us. He says He will help us and uphold us. We need to be firmly established in the fact that God is who He says He is. He is our refuge. Do you know what else God will do for you if you do not fear? See the next verse:

> *"Behold, all they that were incensed against thee shall be ashamed and confounded: they shall be as nothing; and they that strive with thee shall perish"* **(Isaiah 41:10).**

When the devil, your arch-enemy, comes up against you, if you have no fear, he will be ashamed and confounded. He will have to pack his bags and leave. He will have to go and find someone else who will be afraid. Without fear, worry, anxiety, oppression and depression cannot overcome you.

> "In righteousness shalt thou be established: thou shalt be far from oppression; for thou shalt not fear: and from terror; for it shall not come near thee. Behold, they shall surely gather together, but not by me: whosoever shall gather together against thee shall fall for thy sake" **(Isaiah 54: 14-15).**

The above verse confirms to us again that we shall surely be attacked by the enemy. God says here that attacks are not from Him. God does not bring evil against His children. The good news is that if we do not fear, the enemy will fall.

We should remember that no matter how much power the devil thinks he possesses, God is still more powerful. Before the fall of Satan, he was called Lucifer. He was created for good but decided to rebel against God. When you read Isaiah 54:16, please do not be confused about the translation. God is not saying that He created Satan for the purpose of destroying. A better translation should have been, "*I have created the waster **that** destroys.*"

God is reminding us that before becoming Satan, Lucifer was created by Him. God wants us to know that the creature is not greater than the Creator. God knows all about Satan. God knows that Satan's power is limited to affect only those who have fear. That is why God warns us not to have fear. God assures us in verse 17 that no weapon formed against us shall proper.

> *"Behold, I have created the smith that bloweth the coals in the fire, and that bringeth forth an instrument for his work; and I have created the waster to destroy. No weapon that is formed against thee shall prosper; and every tongue that shall rise against thee in judgment thou shalt condemn. This is the heritage of the servants of the LORD, and their righteousness is of me, saith the LORD"* **(Isaiah 54: 16-17).**

The key to realizing all these promises is in verse 14. *"In righteousness shalt thou be established:..."* **(Isaiah 54:14).** If you want to be able to spend your life free from fear, then you must be established in righteousness. I may write a book on righteousness. But for now, please know that righteousness is not the same as holiness. Righteousness is something that God imputes to us. Holiness is what God expects from us. We are already righteous because of the work of our LORD Jesus Christ. You should never think about yourself as a worthless and useless nobody. You were bought by the precious blood of the Son of God.

Chapter 9

<u>It Doesn't All Depend On God You Have A Part To Play</u>

Let us look at one of our foundational scriptures again:

> *"Inasmuch then as the children have partaken of flesh and blood, He Himself likewise shared in the same, that through death He might destroy him who <u>had</u> the power of death, that is, the devil, and release those who through fear of death were all their lifetime subject to bondage"* **(Hebrews 2: 14-15).**

We should note in this verse that Jesus came and "destroyed" the devil. This word "destroy" is often misunderstood by people. Jesus did not eliminate or annihilate the devil. A better translation of the word is "paralyze." Can you see yourself being afraid of someone who is paralyzed? If not, then why would you be afraid of the devil? Why would you be afraid of anything he may want to do to you? Jesus paralyzed the devil to the point where he is no longer capable of harming us unless we bring ourselves into his presence and into his domain. Someone who is paralyzed may not be able to move around or chase you around. But if you bring yourself close to that person, he could still hurt you in some ways.

FREEDOM FROM FEAR

Satan uses deception to put fear into our hearts and cause us to disobey God's Word. Some people claim they have phobias. Phobias are nothing but fear that the enemy has put into their hearts. Why should we be afraid of heights, airplanes, tall buildings, cats (especially black cats) and all the other phobias we might say we have? Why should we be afraid of the dark? God goes with us everywhere, including the dark. We need to overcome those phobias and remember that Jesus penetrated the dark world. He went to hell itself where death and Satan were and paralyzed the devil. The devil is like a toothless bull-dog and an old toothless roaring lion. Jesus delivered us who through the fear of death were all our lifetime subject to the devil.

Satan rules the world through fear. But Jesus went through death so that He might deliver us from the bondage of fear. You and I are no longer subject to the bondage of fear, because Jesus has delivered us. He gave us the spirit of love. Perfect love casts out fear. Where there is no fear, there is no path for Satan to enter into our lives. I used to be in bondage and fear had a grip on my life. But I am no longer in bondage. I am delivered. If you are born again, then you must realize that you have been delivered from the bondage of fear.

Anytime you are afraid, you must remember that you are listening to the devil. When you act on that fear, you must remember that you are acting on the words of the devil. Your acting on fear provides an access to Satan to come into your life and cause trouble. Remember that Satan has no authority unless we give it to him. Let me repeat again that the Bible says we should give no place to the devil. It means he has no place unless we give it to him.

We have been washed and redeemed by the Blood of the Lamb. That makes us clean. We have a different and new covenant with God. Jesus came to complete the old covenant and to start a new and far better one. You and I can come directly to God and not have to wait for a priest or a preacher. We have a direct line to God through Jesus Christ. Jesus is our direct line to God. There is never a busy tone on God's direct line. There is no call-waiting. There is no voice response unit playing; "If you want God the Father, press 1, if you want Jesus, press 2, if you want the Holy Spirit, press 3 or hold the line for the next operator angel!" No, God answers the phone on your first ring.

Religion comes along and says, "If God wills it, then it will happen." Religion says, "Que Sera, Sera, whatever will be will be!" That is just a big excuse. It is a big "cop out." Why would we even care to do anything in this world if everything depends on God? Why don't we just sit at home and fold our arms? If it is God's will to feed us, then maybe He will bring the food. If it is God's will to bless us with money, then maybe He will cause someone to knock on our doors and bring us a bag of money. If it all depends on God, then let us just go our merry ways and party hearty, because "Que Sera, Sera! Whatever will be, will be."

When someone dies, I'm sure you've heard people, even some preachers, say that "it was their time to go." They often say, "we will all go when it is our time to go." Some even go as far ignorantly as to say; "God took them home." They make other ignorant statements like; "God picked a flower from His garden. God needed them more in heaven than He needs them on earth."

No, no, no, no, no! That is all religion, not Christianity. God is a "Giver," not a "Taker." The Bible says Jesus came to paralyze the one who comes to steal, kill and destroy. Religion is based on a bunch of rules. Christianity is based on acting on the solid Word of God. Religion and tradition will nullify the Word of God. Religion and tradition will cancel the effect of the Word of God in our lives. It is a terrible thing to imagine that anything in this world can nullify God's Word. But, religion will do that. Tradition will do that.

You are wasting your time if you come to church every Sunday just because it is your tradition or simply because you want others to think that you are a Christian. Some people just show up in church once a week as a duty or obligation. They are not really interested in changing or improving themselves. They are not really interested in developing a relationship with Jesus Christ around His Word. Some of them come to church so that when they die, the church can bury them and say good things about them.

True Christians are always hungry for more of God. They are always seeking a closer walk with God. They come to church to worship out of a sincere heart and truly wanting to learn and grow. True Christians don't ever say "I've heard that before." They want to hear more about Jesus. They hunger and thirst for righteousness. Even when they hear the same story over and over and over again, God reveals more things to them out of the same story. Every time you read a certain passage of scripture again, it is possible for God to show you a different picture about Himself or about some area of your life. God's Word is loaded with lots of revelation. We haven't even scratched the surface of the wealth and treasure hidden in God's Word. We need to continue digging into the Word.

Chapter 10

<u>The Fear of Rejection</u>

Please study the account of Cain and Abel. It is recorded that God accepted the offering of Abel and rejected the offering of Cain. Cain was afraid that he himself would be rejected by God just like his offering was. That fear of embarrassment and rejection caused so much anger in Cain that he killed his brother. The fear of rejection resulted in murder.

Many people today live under the fear of rejection. If you are secure with your identity and know who you are in God, then it does not matter what anyone says or thinks about you. You will not be afraid of rejection. But if you are one of those people who are afraid of rejection, then the devil will help you to imagine false things that people might be thinking about you. You will make up things in your mind and believe that is what people are saying or thinking about you. Please let me advise you to quickly repent and drop that fear of rejection. If you continue to live with the fear of rejection, that fear could become bitterness and hatred. You could end up with murder like Cain.

Do you remember what Jesus said about murder? You can be guilty of murder without physically killing anyone. You may be surprised to know that we have Christians who are murderers, sitting in churches. Some Christians have the fear of not measuring up, the fear of not being accepted or the fear of being rebuked and corrected. If you are not careful, such a fear can turn you into a murderer.

Remember that God rebuked and corrected Cain. But instead of receiving God's correction and changing his attitude, Cain's fear of rejection turned into hatred and murder. The first record of killing in the Bible was the result of fear.

> *"And the LORD said unto Cain, Why art thou wroth? and why is thy countenance fallen? If thou doest well, shalt thou not be accepted? and if thou doest not well, sin lieth at the door. And unto thee shall be his desire, and thou shalt rule over him"* **(Genesis 4: 6-7)**.

As children of God, we should never be afraid of rejection. Many church splits are caused by the fear of rejection and the fear of correction. We should remember that God is on our side. We are accepted of God. We should not fear anything that anyone may think about us. Sometimes, we have fear and anxiety simply because we think others will find out who we really are on the inside. Most of our fears come because we are afraid to face the truth. Even though excellence should be our goal, we need to admit the fact that we are normal human beings. We will make mistakes sometimes. This attitude will relieve us of the fear of others finding out that we are not perfect. This will reduce our fear of rejection.

The Fear of Rejection

Many marriages are broken because of fear. "I'm afraid that she doesn't love me anymore." "I'm afraid that he doesn't love me anymore." Do you remember how the devil gains access into your life? It is through fear. In marriage, the road to divorce often starts with a question, which leads to fear.

The non-Christian world is looking for Christians who don't only talk the talk but walk the walk. The world is fed up with hypocrites. They are looking for us to live according to what we say with our mouths. We should not allow any form of fear into our lives. We should listen to God instead of the devil. If you listen to the devil, he will feed your mind with many questions but no answers. Then you will become frustrated, confused and afraid because you don't have answers to your questions.

You may begin to ask questions like, "Where was he the other day?" "Where was she the other day?" "Why did he come home so late?" You are afraid that your spouse might have been doing something bad. You may begin to develop the fear of rejection. This could turn into bitterness and anger and ultimately turn to murder.

Chapter 11

Don't Blame Others

In the book of 1st Samuel, Israel desires and asks God for a king. God told them they did not need a king because He had given them the prophets. But Israel pushed Samuel, who was the prophet of the LORD, and persisted until God gave them a king. We often under-estimate the authority that God has given to us as human beings. We need to remember that God will often grant us desires that we persistently ask Him. If everything was up to God, Israel would not have had a King – at least not at the time they wanted one.

Please be encouraged to study all of 1st Samuel Chapter 15. Saul was Israel's first king. God gave Saul an order for Israel to do specific things. God instructed him to go and destroy the people of Amalek. God gave detailed instructions on how to proceed and what to do. They were to destroy everything and only keep the silver and gold that was to be placed in the temple.

> *"Now go and smite Amalek, and utterly destroy all that they have, and spare them not; but slay both man and woman, infant and suckling, ox and sheep, camel and ass"* **(I Samuel 15:3).**

Saul disobeyed God's Word. He decided he would keep the king alive. He also kept the best of the livestock.

> *"But Saul and the people spared Agag, and the best of the sheep, and of the oxen, and of the fatlings, and the lambs, and all that was good, and would not utterly destroy them:..."*
> **(I Samuel 15:9)**

In some cases, God allowed the Israelites to keep a defeated king alive and bring him back and display him in a victory match as proof that the enemy was truly defeated. But this time, God specifically told Saul to destroy the king of the Amalekites. Saul disobeyed God's instructions.

God told Samuel that He was angry about Saul's disobedience. So Samuel went out to meet Saul and to confront him. But as soon as Saul sees Samuel, he said, *"Blessed be thou of the LORD: I have performed the commandment of the LORD"* **(I Samuel 15:13)**.

Saul began to lie, on top of his disobedience. Some Christians today sound just like Saul. When they come to church, they put up their best smiles and greet everyone with sayings like, *"Praise the LORD, everybody! Halleluiah! Glory to God!"* There is no telling what some of those Christians did during the week.

Even when Samuel confronted Saul with the evidence of the bleating of the sheep, Saul still continued to deny and then began to shift the blame to the people.

> *"And Samuel said, What meaneth then this bleating of the sheep in mine ears, and the lowing of the oxen which I hear?*

Don't Blame Others

*And Saul said, They have brought them
from the Amalekites: for the people
spared the best of the sheep and of the
oxen, to sacrifice unto the LORD thy God;
and the rest we have utterly destroyed"*
(I Samuel 15: 14-15).

Saul would not admit that he disobeyed
God. He became defensive and began to
rationalize his actions, just like some of us do
today. We often come up with flimsy reasons to
justify our disobedience. If we continue to disobey
God's voice and begin to listen to the devil, we
may begin to think that what we are doing is
right. We come to church and use the popular
expressions like, *"Praise the LORD! Glory to God! I
am blessed! I love you Brother! I love you Sister! I
am doing all that God tells me to do."* Deep down
in our hearts, we know we are in disobedience in
some area of our lives.

Saul even thought he could convince
Samuel by saying that the people brought the
livestock to sacrifice to Samuel's God.

*"But the people took of the spoil, sheep
and oxen, the chief of the things which
should have been utterly destroyed, to
sacrifice unto the LORD thy God in Gilgal"*
(I Samuel 15:21).

Do you remember what happened in the
Garden of Eden? Adam refused to accept
responsibility for his actions. He blamed God. He
said, *"It's the woman who you gave me."* Saul
said, *"It's not my fault, it's the people who took the*

livestock." Who is the boss here? The people or Saul?

> *"And Samuel said, Hath the LORD as great delight in burnt offerings and sacrifices, as in obeying the voice of the LORD? Behold, to obey is better than sacrifice, and to hearken than the fat of rams"* **(I Samuel 15:22).**

We should remember that God is not pleased with our sacrifices if we are in disobedience to His Word. You can forget about your sacrifices and good deeds if you are not obeying God's Word. Notice that things got even more serious in verse 23. Samuel said, *"rebellion is as the sin of witchcraft..."* **(I Samuel 15:23).**

Can you imagine that we have many people sitting in churches who are practicing witchcraft? Have you ever been guilty of the sin of witchcraft? You might say, "I am not a witch. I don't have a crystal ball." Well, are you rebellious against something that the pastor teaches from the Word of God? Are you in anger and rebellion against authority or anything that is going on in the church? The Word says rebellion is as the sin of witchcraft! Are you stubborn? The Word says, *"... stubbornness is as iniquity and idolatry"* **(I Samuel 15:23).**

Saul wasn't only disobedient and rebellious. He was also stubborn. Three different times, he said he hadn't done anything wrong. Instead of accepting our faults and repenting, we often insist that we have only done what is right. We blame it on other people in the church. We blame it on other people in our families. We need to remember that disobedience and stubbornness carry very serious consequences. Samuel told Saul that God had rejected him because of his disobedience.

> "....Because thou hast rejected the word of the LORD, he hath also rejected thee from being king" **(I Samuel 15:23).**

Instead of repenting quickly and changing our ways, we often wait until it is too late. We often wait until the devil performs some havoc in our lives before we realize we are on the wrong path. The time for Saul to have changed was when Samuel first came to him. But Saul waited until the judgment was pronounced on him before he said he was wrong.

As soon as the Holy Spirit reveals some area of sin in our lives, we should repent quickly. We should not wait until calamity strikes. We should not wait until we end up in prison. Our disobedience opens the door to the devil to act in our lives. Sometimes, it is our wrong fear of God. When we commit sin, we should not be afraid to run to God.

It is easy for us to want to change once we are in the middle of crises. That type of repentance is called "prison religion." After the judgment was pronounced upon Saul, he developed a "prison religion." Some people truly get born again and change their lives while in prison. But a lot of people just develop "prison religion." They behave well because they know that their good behavior might get them out of jail early. Saul now admits he is wrong because he thinks he can get out of the punishment. After all the earlier denials, he now says:

> "....I have sinned: for I have transgressed the commandment of the LORD, and thy words: because I feared the people, and obeyed their voice. Now therefore, I pray thee, pardon my sin, and turn again with me, that I may worship the LORD"
> **(I Samuel 15: 24-25).**

Did you notice what Saul identified as the cause of his disobedience? Fear! He said he feared the people. Fear is the door, the path, the way for Satan to do what he wants to do in our lives. Saul may not be telling the whole truth here. He might have gone along with the people's wishes because bringing King Agag back alive would have given him some glory. It might have been true that the people put pressure on him, but if he really wanted to, he could have told the people what to do instead of listening to what the people told him to do. He was the king. We should not fear the opinion of people. If you are doing what God wants you to do, then it doesn't matter what people think. We are to follow God, not men. We should give higher reverence to God than to men.

Saul's confession and pleading to Samuel came too late.

> "And Samuel said unto Saul, I will not return with thee: for thou hast rejected the

word of the LORD, and the LORD hath rejected thee from being king over Israel. And as Samuel turned about to go away, he laid hold upon the skirt of his mantle, and it rent. And Samuel said unto him, The LORD hath rent the kingdom of Israel from thee this day, and hath given it to a neighbour of thine, that is better than thou. And also the Strength of Israel will not lie nor repent: for he is not a man, that he should repent" **(I Samuel 15: 26-29).**

Chapter 12

God's Promises Are Dependable

I encourage you to read the familiar story of Moses and the Israelites in Numbers 13. Moses brought the Israelites out from Pharaoh's bondage in Egypt. They came right up to the edge of the Promised Land, the Land of Canaan. We should remember that God had promised their forefathers Abraham, Isaac and Jacob that the land would be theirs. God swore to Abraham that the land would belong to him and his seed and his seed's seed. There is a lot of disturbance in the Middle East about who owns which land. If you read your Bible, you will not have any questions about who owns what.

God clearly said the seed of Abraham who came through Isaac would own the land. God said He would provide for Ishmael, but God did not promise the land to Ishmael and his seed. God only promised the land to the seed of Isaac. The children of Israel came out of Isaac and the Arab nations came out of Ishmael. So there should be no confusion about who owns the land. Israel does! We can argue all we want. People can fight all the wars they want to fight. But in the end, it will turn out exactly as God said it would.

The small nation of Israel has been able to stand against some of the world's most powerful armies. They know God is on their side. Therefore they are not afraid. There are only a few nations in the world that stand behind the nation of Israel. I am glad that our United States of America is one of those few nations.

I can assure you that the nation of Israel is in good hands. Don't even worry about them. God has already decreed what is going to happen. Don't get in fear over the nation of Israel. We should pray for them because God says in His Word that we should pray for the nation of Israel. But don't cry for them because they will be protected by the Almighty Hand of God.

There was a story published from 1967 about Israel's Six Day War. One of the nations who were fighting against the Israelites noticed that anytime they fired their big guns towards Israel, their bullets either fell too short or landed too far from their targets. They were never able to hit any of the targets belonging to the Israelites. The army that was shooting those big guns got so frustrated and puzzled that they jumped out of their tanks and ran away.

The story continued to report that the army of Israel got hold of those tanks and the big guns and fired them back at the enemy. Those same guns hit all their targets very accurately. I don't care how anyone explains away this mystery. You can believe what you want to believe. But I want you to know that it was the angels of God that diverted those guns. One Christian leader is reported to have said that God gave him a vision of what happened that day. He said there were big angels playing with the bullets. Anytime the enemies fired their guns toward Israel, one angel knocked one bullet down too short and another angel pulled other bullets too far beyond the target.

Please listen! The Bible said that we believers have angels on assignment on our behalf. They are fighting battles in the spirit world on our behalf. The Word says in Psalm 91:11 that God shall give His angels charge over us, to keep us in all our ways. God says in Hebrews 1:14 that angels are ministering spirits sent forth to minister for us who are heirs of salvation. If you are born again, I hope you realize that you are an heir of salvation and a joint heir with Jesus. Angels will do for you what they did for Jesus.

Let us continue with our story of Moses and the Israelites. They had just been delivered out of the hands of Egypt, the most powerful nation at that time. Here they are at the entrance of the land God had promised to them through their forefathers. God had told them to go in and possess that land. It did not matter whether some other people were living in the land. God said it belonged to the Israelites. God instructed Moses to select representatives from the twelve tribes and send them ahead to check out the land.

The spies went into the Land of Canaan and saw it flowing with milk and honey, just as God had said. They even brought back some of the extra large fruits to show as proof. But let's pick up their story from verse 28.

"Nevertheless the people be strong that dwell in the land, and the cities are walled, and very great: and moreover we saw the children of Anak there. The Amalekites dwell in the land of the south: and the Hittites, and the Jebusites, and the Amorites, dwell in the mountains: and the Canaanites dwell by the sea, and by the coast of Jordan. And Caleb stilled the people before Moses, and said, Let us go up at once, and possess it; for we are well able to overcome it. But the men that went up with him said, We be not able to go up against the people; for they are stronger than we" **(Numbers 13: 28-31).**

What caused the men to say they were not able? How could the Israelites conclude that the people were stronger than them when they had never tried to fight them? Their statement "*We be not able*" was born out of fear. What they saw with their eyes produced fear in their hearts. This fear produced the wrong words out their mouths.

This is what happens to us, even Christians, today when we look at our physical circumstances with our physical eyes instead of our eyes of faith. The devil whispers into our ears, telling us that we are not able to win the battle in front of us. The devil told the Israelites that they were not able. This produced fear in their hearts.

Notice that the Bible says it is evil for us to make bad confessions. The Bible said the Israelites brought an "evil" report. Fear produces an evil report in us. Fear sometimes causes us to make very ridiculous and stupid statements. The spies said the land eats up its inhabitants. This statement doesn't even make sense at all. If the land eats up anyone who gets in it, why didn't the land eat them up? Why were they able to come back alive?

> "And they brought up an evil report of the land which they had searched unto the children of Israel, saying, The land, through which we have gone to search it, is a land that eateth up the inhabitants thereof; and all the people that we saw in it are men of a great stature"
> **(Numbers 13:32).**

Fear makes us have a very low self-esteem. It makes us think of ourselves as too small to fight. Once we begin to think of ourselves in that way, then we are already defeated. Look at what the Israelites said of themselves in verse 33.

> "And there we saw the giants, the sons of Anak, which come of the giants: and we were in our own sight as grasshoppers, and so we were in their sight"
> **(Numbers 13:33).**

Our evil report about ourselves brings despair and opens the door for the enemy to come in and cause havoc in our lives. The Israelites had so much despair that they started to cry. That is what fear does to all of us. Why do we cry? We cry because we have already concluded that we are not able to win the fight.

"And all the congregation lifted up their voice, and cried; and the people wept that night" (Numbers 14:1-2).

Notice the order in which the devil works. He first puts fear in our hearts. Then we start making bad confessions. Then we despair and give up. That gives the devil the chance to get into our lives and do whatever he wants to do. Notice what comes after the crying. Murmuring! We often start murmuring against our leaders. Fear in our hearts starts a chain reaction, with one evil thing after another. After their murmuring, they started wishing they had died in Egypt. Fear sometimes makes us wish we had died or that we were never born.

"And all the children of Israel murmured against Moses and against Aaron: and the whole congregation said unto them, Would God that we had died in the land of Egypt! or would God we had died in this wilderness!" (Numbers 14:2).

Obviously, the Israelites appear to be totally confused. They were not really telling the truth. Why would they wish they were dead? If they truly meant what they were saying, then why did they run away from Pharaoh's army when the sea opened up for them? Why didn't they just stand there and be slaughtered? They really didn't want to die, but fear caused them to start saying things about themselves that they truly didn't want to happen. Once you open the door for Satan, he will come in and start leading you down the wrong path. It will take the Word of God to drive him out and shut that door.

We need to be very careful about the words we speak. We need to be careful about the bad confessions we make. God tells us in His Word that it will be unto us according to what we have spoken out of our mouths.

One thing that is very surprising about these Israelites is the fact that they had just seen the mighty hand of God deliver them from the most powerful nation of Egypt. They just saw God open up the Red Sea and create dry land for them to walk through. They just saw God close back the sea and destroy the mighty Egyptian army. Just a short while ago, they were singing a song of praise to the LORD for destroying the Egyptians. The following is a part of their song recorded in Exodus:

> "Then sang Moses and the children of Israel this song unto the LORD, and spake, saying, I will sing unto the LORD, for he hath triumphed gloriously: the horse and his rider hath he thrown into the sea. The LORD is my strength and song, and he is become my salvation: he is my God, and I will prepare him an habitation; my father's God, and I will exalt him. The LORD is a man of war: the LORD is his name. Pharaoh's chariots and his host hath he cast into the sea: his chosen captains also are drowned in the Red sea. The depths have covered them:

they sank into the bottom as a stone"
(Exodus 15: 1-5).

These same Israelites were the people who saw God bring water out of a rock for them to drink. They saw God rain bread and meat from heaven to feed them. How could they forget all of God's goodness so soon? How ungrateful! How could they say they are not able? The people of Canaan that they were facing were nowhere nearly as strong as the nation of Egypt. Did they think the God who delivered them from Egypt could not deliver them from these people?

Chapter 13

You Are A Little Jesus

Are we any different from the Israelites? How quickly do we forget God's blessings and His mercy when we face challenges? Whenever we get into fear, don't we quickly forget past victories? It was fear that caused the Israelites to forget that God was on their side. You and I, today, don't only have God on our side. We have a God who lives inside us. We have a better covenant than that of the old covenant. Yes, God is still for us. God is still on our side. But more importantly, God has made His home inside us. Hallelujah! He is working out His purpose and His plan in us from our inside. We need to cooperate with Him.

The power that allowed Jesus, the man, to be victorious while He was on earth, was the fact that He knew God dwelt inside Him. He told Philip that anyone who has seen Him has seen the Father.

> "Jesus saith unto him, Have I been so long time with you, and yet hast thou not known me, Philip? He that hath seen me hath seen the Father; and how sayest thou then, Shew us the Father"
> (John 14:9).

You and I are like Jesus on the earth. Each of us is a little Jesus. God dwells in us. He has made all of His power available to us on the inside. The more we discover from His Word who

He has already made us to be, the less fear we will allow in our hearts. When we face challenges, we will declare that *"Greater is He who is in me than he who is in the world"* **(I John 4:4).** Like Jesus, we should declare to Satan and to the world, *"When you see me, you see God."* We should also declare that, *"I and the Father are one."* The Bible says that the hope of our glory is the fact that Christ is in us.

> *"Even the mystery which hath been hid from ages and from generations, but now is made manifest to His saints: To whom God would make known what is the riches of the glory of this mystery among the Gentiles; which is Christ in you, the hope of glory"* **(Colossians 1:26-27).**

We should rejoice in who God has made us to be. We should rejoice in the fact that God is in us. God is love, and perfect love casts out fear. There should be no room for fear in our hearts. Instead of Jesus having no room at the inn, the devil should have no room at the inn of our hearts. We are the temple of the Holy Spirit.

> *"What? know ye not that your body is the temple of the Holy Ghost which is in you, which ye have of God, and ye are not your own?"* **(I Corinthians 6:9).**

Jesus did what He did because He knew that God lived in Him. God lives in us also. That is the reason we are who He says we are. That is the reason we can do what He says we can do. God is alive in me! The Godhead is alive in me! You must realize that God is alive in you today!

You Are A Little Jesus

God wants to continue the ministry of Jesus through you. But before He can do that, you must give Him permission. You must have the same assurance as Jesus did, that God is alive in you. You must accept the fact that *"as He is, so are we in the world" (I John 4:17).* You are a little Jesus! The Bible says we are gods *(Psalms 82:6* and *John 10:34).* If you are still not convinced, please look at part of the prayer that Jesus prayed to the Father in John Chapter 17:

> *"As thou hast sent me into the world, even so have I also sent them into the world. And for their sakes I sanctify myself, that they also might be sanctified through the truth. Neither pray I for these alone, but for them also which shall believe on me through their word; That they all may be one; as thou, Father, art in me, and I in thee, that they also may be one in us: that the world may believe that thou hast sent me. And the glory which thou gavest me I have given them; that they may be one, even as we are one: I in them, and thou in me, that they may be made perfect in one; and that the world may know that thou hast sent me, and hast loved them, as thou hast loved me" (John 17: 18-23).*

Please remember that in the beginning, God made man in His image and in His likeness. You and I are little gods *(Psalms 82:6* and *John 10:34)..* You and I are just as one in God as Jesus is one in God. Jesus is in me. I am in Jesus. Jesus is in God the Father. God the Father is in Jesus. We are all one in Him. God the Father loves me with the same love with which He loved His Son Jesus. Since perfect love casts out fear, that love in me will not allow fear in my life. And if there is no room for fear, then there is no room for Satan to get in. There is no room for him at the inn.

The main reason the children of Israel got into fear at the sight of the giants is that they forgot who they were and whose they were. They forgot who was on their side. They forgot the God who got them out of the land of Egypt and performed miracles among them.

How long do we have to remain in bondage before we realize that Jesus has set us free? Jesus went through death on our behalf so that He would set us free. We are no longer in bondage. The only time that we start going back into bondage is when we start listening to the devil instead of listening to God. We need to continue in our fellowship with God. We need to get a better understanding of who we are in God. We need to remember that God is in us. That is the only way we can keep fear out of our lives.

Chapter 14

__Be Strong and Of Good Courage__

What was the first thing that God commanded Joshua? God told Joshua not to fear. Be strong. Be of good courage. Courage is the opposite of fear. If you want to have victory in your life, you must not have any fear. Without fear, the enemy cannot get in. If you have fear, then the thing that you fear will come upon you. If fear knocks at your door, don't let him in.

"Be strong and of a good courage: for unto this people shalt thou divide for an inheritance the land, which I sware unto their fathers to give them. Only be thou strong and very courageous, that thou mayest observe to do according to all the law, which Moses my servant commanded thee: turn not from it to the right hand or to the left, that thou mayest prosper whithersoever thou goest. This book of the law shall not depart out of thy mouth; but thou shalt meditate therein day and night, that thou mayest observe to do according to all that is written therein: for then thou shalt make thy way prosperous, and then thou shalt have good success. Have not I commanded thee? Be strong and of a good courage; be not afraid, neither be thou dismayed: for the LORD thy God is with thee whithersoever thou goest
(Joshua 1:6-9).

85

Please pay attention to some of the key words in the above passage. God said "**only** be strong and very courageous." This means there are no options. It is not a little courage and a little fear. It is not 99% courage and 1% fear. It must be 100% courage. From the passage, whose responsibility is it for you to prosper? It s yours! It is God's will for you to prosper. But He is not just going to dump prosperity on you while you fold your hands and do nothing or live any kind of life you want to live.

God said, you will make your way prosperous and you will have good success. God does not lie. If you fulfill the conditions, you will get the results. If you meditate on God's Word day and night, and do according to all that is written in the Word, you will be prosperous. You will have good success. Most people in church are waiting on God to make them prosperous. We should not wait for God because He is waiting for us. God is always ready to move whenever we are ready for Him to move.

Notice in verse 9 that God repeats the command to Joshua against fear. God said "...be not afraid." This was the primary condition for Joshua to be able to deliver the Promised Land to the Children of Israel. Why did the first generation of the children of Israel not make it to the Promised Land? They were afraid! If you want to win the battles in your life, then you must not have any fear. Without fear, you will allow God to do everything in your life that He has promised.

But with fear, you allow the devil to do anything in your life that he wants to do. Do you remember what the devil wants to do in your life? Steal, Kill and Destroy!

Look at the effects of "fear" in the life of Job:

> "And it was so, when the days of their feasting were gone about, that Job sent and sanctified them, and rose up early in the morning, and offered burnt offerings according to the number of them all: for Job said, It may be that my sons have sinned, and cursed God in their hearts. Thus did Job continually" **(Job 1:5)**.

The scripture said Job offered sacrifices every morning on behalf of each of his sons. Every morning! Why did he do that? He said, "it **_may be_** that my sons have sinned and cursed God in their hearts." Doesn't that sound like he had fear? Doesn't that sound like he was overly worried about his children? He said, "it **_may be_**..." He was not offering burnt offerings out of faith. He was doing it out of fear.

Job's fear opened the door and gave access to the devil to destroy his children. Once the devil comes into your life, he doesn't just stop at one thing. He continues to cause havoc in other areas of your life. After destroying Job's children, the devil destroyed Job's property. Almost everything in Job's life was wiped out in just a very short time. In chapter 2, we notice that Satan came back and put nasty boils over Job's body. It was so bad that his wife challenged him to just go ahead and curse God and die.

It is obvious that Job did not understand the love of God. Job did not have the Bible like we have it today. He did not know that only good and perfect gifts come down from above from our Father of Love. Job thought that both good and evil came from God. We need to realize that God inspired the writers of scripture to include certain things just for us to learn from. It does not mean that every statement made by everyone in the Bible is the truth. Job was very sincere. He did not want to sin against God with his lips. He was sincere, but he was sincerely wrong. [Another place that Job was sincerely wrong was when he said *"God giveth and God taketh away."* God is a giver and not a taker.]

In all of chapter 3, Job starts to curse the day he was born. Some people read the Book of Job and blame God for turning Satan loose to harm Job. That is a lie of the devil. God will never team up with Satan to hurt any of His children. If you came to my house and saw that I was encouraging a big bull-dog to attack one of my children, what would you call me? A child-abuser!

If you have children, will you break one of their legs in order to teach them something? Will you burn their house down, or cause them to have a car wreck in order to teach them something? Will you take all their money away from them in order to keep them humble? But that is exactly what we often blame God for. We say God brings sickness and poverty on us in order to teach us and keep us humble.

The devil has blinded the eyes of some Christians to make them think that God is their problem. The Bible doesn't teach us that God is our problem. The Bible teaches us that God is our answer. God is our refuge. A very present help in the time of trouble. Jesus is The Way, The Truth, and The Life. His name is The Way <u>out</u> of trouble. He is not The Way <u>into</u> trouble.

Do you want to know the real truth about what happened to Job? Job himself told us. Towards the end of that chapter, Job reveals the real reason all that calamity came upon him. He said it was because of **fear**.

> *"For the thing which I greatly feared is come upon me, and that which I was afraid of is come unto me"* **(Job 3:25)**.

If you continue in fear, whatever you fear will come upon you. Thank God that He has delivered us from fear. In the presence of fear, we can trust in the LORD. In the midst of fear, we can remember the Words of the LORD and trust in those Words rather than the words of the devil. We can trust that the LORD will deliver us from every situation that is facing us.

Final Words and Proclamation

The Bible says we have been made kings and priests. God has come to live inside us. We are the temple of the Holy Spirit. God is not just for us and with us. He is in us. We should obey the Word of God. We should not listen to people who do not draw us towards God. We should not listen to the devil.

It is up to you and me to have faith in God instead of the fear of the devil. We have been delivered from fear. God is a Good God. We serve a BIG GOD! We are not playing church. We are serious! This is the time to be what God has made us to be. God has done His part. He has done all that He needs to do. The ball is in your court.

My prayer for you is that you will maintain your freedom from fear and live a life of victory. We should always be moving in faith instead of fear. Faith is trusting God's Word. Faith doesn't ask questions. Faith makes declarations of what God has already said in His Word. Faith proclaims!

I recommend that on a regular basis, especially in times when you are tempted to be afraid, you make the following declarations out loud. These proclamations should come out of your heart and not just your mouth.

"Jesus has delivered me from the power of fear. He has delivered me

from the power of the devil himself. I am free! I am free!! I am delivered from fear forever! I will not be put back into bondage again to fear. I have received the spirit of adoption. Therefore I cry, 'Aba Father.'

God has not given me the spirit of fear. He has given me the spirit of Power, and of Love and of a Sound Mind. The LORD is my light. He is my salvation. Of whom shall I be afraid? I will not fear. The LORD is the strength of my life. Of whom shall I be afraid? I will not be afraid. I am not afraid of any man. I am not afraid of the opinions of men.

Jesus has set me free. I am developed in love. Therefore I cast out fear. There is no fear in me. No more fear of sickness. No more fear of accidents. No more fear of terrorists. No more fear of lack. No more fear of the future. God has delivered me from all my fears! God has delivered me from all my fears!! God has delivered me from all my fears!!! No more fear! No more fear!! No more fear in me!!! Whenever I am afraid, I will trust in God. Hallelujah!!!

"Greater is He who is in me. Than he that is in the world. The Greater One lives in me. He puts me over. I cannot fail. Because the Greater one lives in me. I have His ability. For me to fail, God will have to fail. God cannot fail. Therefore I cannot fail. Hallelujah!

"I dwell in the secret place of the Most High. I abide under the shadow of the Almighty. A thousand shall fall at my side, and ten thousand shall fall at my right hand. But it will not come near me. There is no fear in me. I will get on airplanes and not be afraid. I will climb into tall buildings if I need to and will not be afraid. I am not afraid of terrorists. No fear here! No fear here!! No fear here! My God is faithful to His Word, Hallelujah!"

Call To Salvation

Fear is one of the reasons people do not want to give their lives to God and be born again. They are afraid that they might not be able to live the life of a Christian. After reading a book like this one, or after hearing a good sermon, you might be inspired to surrender your life to Jesus. But the devil will come and whisper into your ears, "You can't live that Christian life."

Living the Christian life is not all about you. It is about Jesus coming to live inside you and living the life through you. If you could have lived the Christian life all by yourself, then there would have been no need for Jesus to come and die for you. There would have been no need for the Holy Spirit. He needs your cooperation, but living the Christian life does not depend on your own power. The Holy Spirit who lives in your heart will give you the power to be what you are not able to be on your own. He will give you the ability to do what you are not able to do on your own. You can do all things through Christ who strengthens you.

Please let me encourage you to search your heart. Is the Holy Spirit calling you today to a life of surrender? If you have never asked Jesus Christ to come into your life, then today is your day. He is waiting at your heart's door and knocking. He will not force Himself into your heart. Please open your heart's door and allow

Him to come in. He will change your life. You do not need to be clean before coming to Him. He will clean you up. If you are on drugs, you do not need to quit before coming to Jesus. If you are in some terrible sin today, or if you are addicted to alcohol, you do not need to wait until you get sober.

Some of you who read this book may have accepted the LORD at one time in the past. But you have not allowed the Holy Spirit to guide your life. You turned your back on Him. If that is you, then please allow me to encourage you also to surrender your life completely to Him. He will restore the joy of your salvation. He will give you a fresh start.

If you belong to any of these two categories, then please listen to the words of the following song:

> "Come unto Jesus, while you have time.
> Come just as you are, don't delay.
> Can't you hear the Spirit calling?
> Come, taste and see that the LORD is good.
> Come, receive new life.
> Come, receive everlasting life.
> Come, receive strength.
> Come! Come!! Come!!!"

Please say the following prayer out loud to God;

> "Heavenly Father, I come to you in the Name of JESUS. Your Word says in Romans 5:8 that, *"while we were yet sinners, CHRIST died for us."* I realize that I cannot change myself. I am

asking for your help. I am calling on you. I pray and ask JESUS to come into my heart and be LORD over my life. According to Romans 10: 9-10, *"If thou shalt confess with thy mouth the LORD JESUS, and shalt believe in thine heart that God raised Him from the dead, then thou shalt be saved. For with the heart man believeth unto righteousness; and with the mouth confession is made unto salvation."* I do that now. I confess that JESUS is LORD and I believe in my heart that God raised Him from the dead for me.

I am now re-born! I am a Christian – a child of the Almighty God! I am saved! The old life is behind me. I am beginning a brand new life. I am no longer subject to the bondage of fear and death."

Please be sure to share your new-birth experience with someone else. We need to be connected to one another as children of God. Please join a church where the true Word of God is preached. They will love and care for you as you grow spiritually. Being part of a church family increases our strength. It is God's plan for us.

WELCOME TO THE FAMILY!

Bible References

This section contains a summary of the Bible verses used in this book. Please be encouraged to memorize the Word of God and speak it out to yourself on a daily basis. God told Joshua; and God is telling you and me today, that, **"This book of the law shall not depart out of thy mouth; but thou shalt meditate therein day and night, that thou mayest observe to do according to all that is written therein: for then thou shalt make thy way prosperous, and then thou shalt have good success" (Joshua 1:8).**

These verses will help you to maintain your deliverance from fear. Please read them often until they become written on the tablets of your heart. When the devil comes to attack you with fear, then out of the abundance of your heart, your mouth will speak words of faith and victory.

"Now the serpent was more subtle than any beast of the field which the LORD God had made. And he said unto the woman, Yea, hath God said, Ye shall not eat of every tree of the garden? And the woman said unto the serpent, We may eat of the fruit of the trees of the garden: But of the fruit of the tree which is in the midst of the garden, God hath said, Ye shall not

eat of it, neither shall ye touch it, lest ye die. And the serpent said to the woman, Ye shall not surely die. For God knows that in the day ye eat thereof, then your eyes shall be opened, and ye shall be as gods, knowing good and evil. And when the woman saw that the tree was good for food, and that it was pleasant to the eyes, and a tree to be desired to make one wise, she took of the fruit thereof, and did eat, and gave also unto her husband with her; and he did eat. And the eyes of them both were opened, and they knew that they were naked; and they sewed fig leaves together, and made themselves aprons. And they heard the voice of the LORD God walking in the garden in the cool of the day: and Adam and his wife hid themselves from the presence of the LORD God amongst the trees of the garden And the LORD God called unto Adam, and said unto him, Where art thou? And he said, I heard thy voice in the garden, and I was afraid, because I was naked; and I hid myself" **(Genesis 3:1-10)**.

"And the LORD said unto Cain, Why art thou wroth? and why is thy countenance fallen? If thou doest well, shalt thou not be accepted? and if thou

doest not well, sin lieth at the door. And unto thee shall be his desire, and thou shalt rule over him"
(Genesis 4: 6-7).

"Then sang Moses and the children of Israel this song unto the LORD, and spake, saying, I will sing unto the LORD, for he hath triumphed gloriously: the horse and his rider hath he thrown into the sea. The LORD is my strength and song, and he is become my salvation: he is my God, and I will prepare him an habitation; my father's God, and I will exalt him. The LORD is a man of war: the LORD is his name. Pharaoh's chariots and his host hath he cast into the sea: his chosen captains also are drowned in the Red sea. The depths have covered them: they sank into the bottom as a stone" ***(Exodus 15: 1-5).***

*"And all the congregation lifted up their voice, and cried; and the people wept that night"****(Numbers 14:1-2).***

"Nevertheless the people be strong that dwell in the land, and the cities are walled, and very great: and moreover we saw the children of Anak there. The Amalekites dwell in the land of the south: and the Hittites, and the

Jebusites, and the Amorites, dwell in the mountains: and the Canaanites dwell by the sea, and by the coast of Jordan. And Caleb stilled the people before Moses, and said, Let us go up at once, and possess it; for we are well able to overcome it. But the men that went up with him said, We be not able to go up against the people; for they are stronger than we. And they brought up an evil report of the land which they had searched unto the children of Israel, saying, The land, through which we have gone to search it, is a land that eateth up the inhabitants thereof; and all the people that we saw in it are men of a great stature. And there we saw the giants, the sons of Anak, which come of the giants: and we were in our own sight as grasshoppers, and so we were in their sight" *(Numbers 28:33).*

"Be strong and of a good courage: for unto this people shalt thou divide for an inheritance the land, which I sware unto their fathers to give them. Only be thou strong and very courageous, that thou mayest observe to do according to all the law, which Moses my servant commanded thee: turn not from it to the right hand or to the left, that thou mayest prosper whithersoever thou *goest. This book of the law shall not depart out of thy mouth; but thou shalt meditate therein day and night, that thou mayest observe to do according to all that is written therein: for then thou shalt make thy way prosperous, and then thou shalt have good success. Have not I commanded thee? Be strong and of a good courage; be not afraid, neither be thou dismayed: for the LORD thy God is with thee whithersoever thou goest"*

(Joshua 1:6-9).

"Now go and smite Amalek, and utterly destroy all that they have, and spare them not; but slay both man and woman, infant and suckling, ox and sheep, camel and ass"

(I Samuel 15:3).

"But Saul and the people spared Agag, and the best of the sheep, and of the oxen, and of the fatlings, and the lambs, and all that was good, and would not utterly destroy them:."

(I Samuel 15:9).

"Blessed be thou of the LORD: I have performed the commandment of the LORD. And Samuel said, What meaneth then this bleating of the sheep in mine ears, and the lowing of

the oxen which I hear? And Saul said, They have brought them from the Amalekites: for the people spared the best of the sheep and of the oxen, to sacrifice unto the LORD thy God; and the rest we have utterly destroyed. But the people took of the spoil, sheep and oxen, the chief of the things which should have been utterly destroyed, to sacrifice unto the LORD thy God in Gilgal. And Samuel said, Hath the LORD as great delight in burnt offerings and sacrifices, as in obeying the voice of the LORD? Behold, to obey is better than sacrifice, and to hearken than the fat of rams. For rebellion is as the sin of witchcraft, and stubbornness is as iniquity and idolatry. Because thou hast rejected the word of the LORD, he hath also rejected thee from being king. And Saul said unto Samuel, .I have sinned: for I have transgressed the commandment of the LORD, and thy words: because I feared the people, and obeyed their voice. Now therefore, I pray thee, pardon my sin, and turn again with me, that I may worship the LORD. And Samuel said unto Saul, I will not return with thee: for thou hast rejected the word of the LORD, and the LORD hath rejected thee from being king over Israel. And as Samuel turned about to go away, he laid hold upon the skirt of his mantle, and it rent. And Samuel said unto him, The LORD hath rent the kingdom of Israel from thee this day, and hath given it to a neighbour of thine, that is better than thou. And also the Strength of Israel will not lie nor repent: for he is not a man, that he should repent"

(I Samuel 15: 13-29).

"And David said unto Saul, Thy servant kept his father's sheep, and there came a lion, and a bear, and took a lamb out of the flock: And I went out after him, and smote him, and delivered it out of his mouth: and when he arose against me, I caught him by his beard, and smote him, and slew him. Thy servant slew both the lion and the bear: and this uncircumcised Philistine shall be as one of them, seeing he hath defied the armies of the living God. David said moreover, The LORD that delivered me out of the paw of the lion, and out of the paw of the bear, he will deliver me out of the hand of this Philistine......."

(I Samuel 17: 34-37).

"And it was so, when the days of their feasting were gone about, that Job sent and sanctified them, and rose up early in the morning, and offered burnt offerings according to the number of them all: for Job said, It may be that my sons have sinned, and cursed God in their hearts. Thus did Job continually" *(Job 1:5)*.

"For the thing which I greatly feared is come upon me, and that which I was afraid of is come unto me" *(Job 3:25)*.

"God is our refuge and strength, a very present help in trouble" *(Psalm 46:1)*.

"The LORD is my shepherd; I shall not want. He makes me to lie down in green pastures; He leads me beside the still waters. He restores my soul; He leads me in the paths of righteousness For His name's sake. Yea, though I walk through the valley of the shadow of death, I will fear no evil; For You are with me; Your rod and Your staff, they comfort me. You prepare a table before me in the presence of my enemies; You anoint my head with oil; My cup runs over. Surely goodness and mercy shall follow me all the days of my life; And I will dwell in the house of the LORD Forever" *(Psalm 23)*.

"The LORD is my light and my salvation; Whom shall I fear? The

LORD is the strength of my life; Of whom shall I be afraid? When the wicked came against me to eat up my flesh, My enemies and foes, They stumbled and fell. Though an army may encamp against me, My heart shall not fear; Though war may rise against me, In this I will be confident" **(Psalm 27: 1-3).**

"For in the time of trouble he shall hide me in his pavilion: in the secret of his tabernacle shall he hide me; he shall set me up upon a rock" **(Psalm 27:5).**

"God is our refuge and strength, A very present help in trouble. Therefore we will not fear, Even though the earth be removed, And though the mountains be carried into the midst of the sea; Though its waters roar and be troubled, Though the mountains shake with its swelling. Selah There is a river whose streams shall make glad the city of God, The holy place of the tabernacle of the Most High. God is in the midst of her, she shall not be moved; God shall help her, just at the break of dawn. The nations raged, the kingdoms were moved; He uttered His voice, the earth melted. The LORD of hosts is with us; The God of Jacob is our refuge. Selah" **(Psalm 46: 1-7).**

"Be merciful to me, O God, for man would swallow me up; Fighting all day he oppresses me. My enemies would hound me all day, For there are many who fight against me, O Most High. Whenever I am afraid, I will trust in You. In God (I will praise His word), In God I have put my trust; I will not fear. What can flesh do to me?"
(Psalm 56: 1-4).

"When I cry out to You, Then my enemies will turn back; This I know, because God is for me. In God (I will praise His word), In the LORD (I will praise His word), In God I have put my trust; I will not be afraid. What can man do to me?" **(Psalm 56: 9-11).**

"He that dwelleth in the secret place of the most High shall abide under the shadow of the Almighty I will say of the LORD, He is my refuge and my fortress: my God; in him will I trust. Surely he shall deliver thee from the snare of the fowler, and from the noisome pestilence. He shall cover thee with his feathers, and under his wings shalt thou trust: his truth shall be thy shield and buckler. Thou shalt not be afraid for the terror by night; nor for the arrow that flieth by day; Nor for the pestilence that walketh in

darkness; nor for the destruction that wasteth at noonday. A thousand shall fall at thy side, and ten thousand at thy right hand; but it shall not come nigh thee. Only with thine eyes shalt thou behold and see the reward of the wicked. Because thou hast made the LORD, which is my refuge, even the most High, thy habitation; There shall no evil befall thee, neither shall any plague come nigh thy dwelling. For he shall give his angels charge over thee, to keep thee in all thy ways. They shall bear thee up in their hands, lest thou dash thy foot against a stone. Thou shalt tread upon the lion and adder: the young lion and the dragon shalt thou trample under feet. Because he hath set his love upon me, therefore will I deliver him: I will set him on high, because he hath known my name. He shall call upon me, and I will answer him: I will be with him in trouble; I will deliver him, and honour him. With long life will I satisfy him, and show him my salvation"

(Psalm 91: 1-16).

"The LORD is on my side; I will not fear: what can man do unto me?"**(Psalm 118:6).**

"...the fear of the LORD is the beginning of knowledge: but fools despise wisdom and instruction....For that they hated knowledge, and did not choose the fear of the LORD. They would none of my counsel: they despised all my reproof. Therefore shall they eat of the fruit of their own way, and be filled with their own devices" **(Proverbs 1: 7, 29-31).**

"For a just man falleth seven times, and riseth up again: but the wicked shall fall into mischief"

(Proverbs 24:16).

"Fear thou not; for I am with thee: be not dismayed; for I am thy God: I will strengthen thee; yea, I will help thee; yea, I will uphold thee with the right hand of my righteousness. Behold, all they that were incensed against thee shall be ashamed and confounded: they shall be as nothing; and they that strive with thee shall perish"

(Isaiah 41: 10-11).

"In righteousness shalt thou be established: thou shalt be far from oppression; for thou shalt not fear: and from terror; for it shall not come near thee. Behold, they shall surely gather together, but not by me: whosoever

shall gather together against thee shall fall for thy sake. Behold, I have created the smith that bloweth the coals in the fire, and that bringeth forth an instrument for his work; and I have created the waster to destroy. No weapon that is formed against thee shall prosper; and every tongue that shall rise against thee in judgment thou shalt condemn. This is the heritage of the servants of the LORD, and their righteousness is of me, saith the LORD" *(Isaiah 54: 14-17)*.

"Shadrach, Meshach and Abednego answered and said to the king, O Nebuchadnezzar, we are not careful to answer thee in this matter. If it be so, our God whom we serve is able to deliver us from the burning fiery furnace, and he will deliver us out of thine hand, O king. But if not, be it known unto thee, O king, that we will not serve thy gods, nor worship the golden image which thou hast set up" *(Daniel 3: 16-18)*.

"The thief cometh not, but for to steal, and to kill, and to destroy: I am come that they might have life, and that they might have it more abundantly" *(John 10:10)*.

"Jesus saith unto him, Have I been so long time with you, and yet hast thou not known me, Philip? He that hath seen me hath seen the Father; and how sayest thou then, Shew us the Father" *(John 14:9)*.

"Abide in me, and I in you. As the branch cannot bear fruit of itself, except it abide in the vine; no more can ye, except ye abide in me" *(John 15:4)*.

"I pray for them: I pray not for the world, but for them which thou hast given me; for they are thine. And all mine are thine, and thine are mine; and I am glorified in them"
(John 17: 9-10).

"As thou hast sent me into the world, even so have I also sent them into the world. And for their sakes I sanctify myself, that they also might be sanctified through the truth. Neither pray I for these alone, but for them also which shall believe on me through their word; That they all may be one; as thou, Father, art in me, and I in thee, that they also may be one in us: that the world may believe that thou hast sent me. And the glory which thou gavest me I have given them; that they may be one, even as we are one: I in them, and thou in me, that they may be made perfect in one; and that the world may know that thou hast sent me, and hast loved them, as thou hast loved me" *(John 17: 18-23)*.

"Faith comes by hearing, and hearing by the Word of God" *(Romans 10:17)*.

"What? know ye not that your body is the temple of the Holy Ghost which is in you, which ye have of God, and ye are not your own?"
(I Corinthians 6:9).

"But the fruit of the Spirit is love, joy, peace, longsuffering, gentleness, goodness, faith, Meekness, temperance: against such there is no law" *(Galatians 5:22)*.

"Neither give place to the devil" *(Ephesians 4:27)*.

"And in nothing be terrified by your adversaries: which is to them an evident token of perdition, but to you of salvation, and that of God"
(Philippians 1:28).

"And do not for a moment be frightened or intimidated in anything by your opponents and adversary. For *such consistency and fearlessness will be a clear sign and proof and seal to them of their impending destruction, but a sure token and evidence of your deliverance and salvation, and that from God"* **(Philippians 1:28 AMP).**

"Even the mystery which hath been hid from ages and from generations, but now is made manifest to his saints: To whom God would make known what is the riches of the glory of this mystery among the Gentiles; which is Christ in you, the hope of glory" **(Colossians 1:26-27).**

"For God has not given us the spirit of fear, but of power and of love and of a sound mind" **(2 Timothy 1:7).**

"Inasmuch then as the children have partaken of flesh and blood, He Himself likewise shared in the same, that through death He might destroy him who <u>had</u> the power of death, that is, the devil, and release those who through fear of death were all their lifetime subject to bondage"

(Hebrews 2: 14-15).

"Greater is He who is in me than he who is in the world" **(I John 4:4).**

Bible References

"He that loveth not knoweth not God; for God is love **(1 John 4:8).**

"There is no fear in love; but perfect love casts out fear, because fear involves torment. He who fears has not been made perfect in love" **(1 John 4:18).**

"Behold I stand at the door and knock. If anyone hears my voice and opens the door, I will come in to him and dine with him" **(Revelation 3:20).**

Ω THE END Ω